—— TRUE TALES OF ——

CALIFORNIA
COASTSIDE
STATE PARKS

TRUE TALES OF
CALIFORNIA COASTSIDE
STATE PARKS

JOANN SEMONES

THE
History
PRESS

Published by The History Press
Charleston, SC
www.historypress.com

Front cover, top left: Año Nuevo Island. *Courtesy of Julie Barrow*; *top center*: the *New York* shipwreck. *Courtesy of San Mateo County History Museum*; *top right*: Burleigh Murray State Park. *Courtesy of Coastside State Parks Association*; *bottom*: Pigeon Point Light Station. *Courtesy of Julie Barrow*.
Back cover: Pebble Beach. *Courtesy of Ingrid Holthuis*.

First published 2022

Manufactured in the United States

ISBN 9781467153034

Library of Congress Control Number: 2022943531

Notice: The information in this book is true and complete to the best of our knowledge. It is offered without guarantee on the part of the author or The History Press. The author and The History Press disclaim all liability in connection with the use of this book.

To Julie Barrow,
a pioneer in her own right

CONTENTS

CONTENTS

INTRODUCTION

This book concentrates on state parks situated close to the California coast between Montara (to the north) and Capitola (to the south). They are located south of San Francisco in San Mateo County and in Santa Cruz County in an area we generally refer to as the Coastside. Each park is different in its development, topography and experience. Yet, taken as a whole, they give us a vivid picture of California's rich and dynamic growth and history.

Inside these pages, you will meet a few key historic personalities. Some are forgotten pioneers and several of the parks are less known than others. Each chapter highlights unusual characters as well as unique industries that helped form our stunning Coastside. You will discover coastal parks, beaches, wildlife preserves, an iconic lighthouse and a concrete ship. You will encounter land barons and speculators, builders, businessmen and lumbermen, naturalists, dairy farmers and ranchers, even a freedom fighter.

The profiles represent several eras, including the Spanish mission period, the gold rush, development of shipping and maritime endeavors, lumbering, dairy farming and more. Some of the people were land speculators, while others worked the land and passed it down through their families. Quite a few were colorful local characters. Each left a distinct imprint on specific properties and on the Coastside as a whole. Not only do the stories of these vibrant people reflect important historical eras, they also continue to fill our imaginations.

Sources and images used in the book include those from the author's collection, newspaper accounts and clips from the California State Library, archives of museums including the San Mateo County History Museum, history books and reference materials, as well as California State Parks historical documents and records.

The book was created after the horrific wildfires of August 2020 that swept through San Mateo and Santa Cruz Counties. Hundreds of fires were ignited as a result of a rare thunderstorm that produced more than eleven thousand bolts of lightning. The skies filled with smoke and ash, turning from gray to orange to black.

The fires lasted more than a month and burned over 86,500 acres, damaging numerous Coastside state parks and many communities nestled in and around them. Miraculously, only one person was killed. It was possible that none of the parks would survive. Today, while some of the parks have recovered, others are struggling to return to their previous condition. For many, the devastation will never fully be rectified.

As a longtime Coastside resident and a dedicated champion of California State Parks, I hope these stories offer an opportunity to reflect on not only the beauty of our parks but also their history. Reaching into the past is both challenging and illuminating. You never know what you will find or what you will learn. It can change your perspective and your feelings. It can fuel your curiosity of the world around you.

When you plan to visit any of the parks, please check beforehand about their hours and what is and is not open to the public. When you arrive, please offer your respects to their past, present and future. You may even consider becoming a volunteer or donor and becoming part of a lasting legacy.

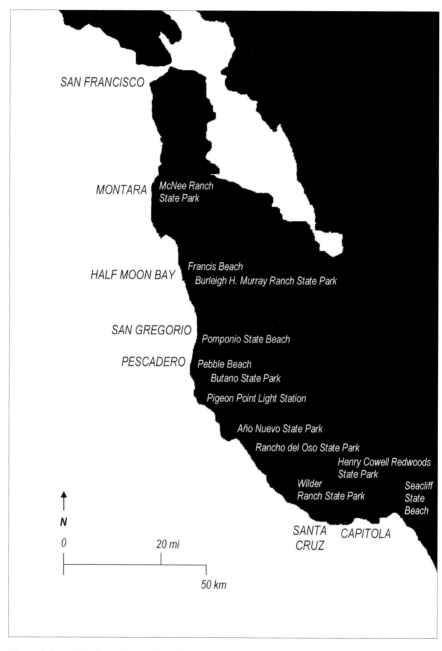

SAN FRANCISCO

MONTARA   McNee Ranch
           State Park

HALF MOON BAY   Francis Beach
                 Burleigh H. Murray Ranch State Park

SAN GREGORIO   Pomponio State Beach

PESCADERO   Pebble Beach
             Butano State Park

             Pigeon Point Light Station

             Año Nuevo State Park
               Rancho del Oso State Park
                 Henry Cowell Redwoods
                   State Park
             Wilder   Seacliff
             Ranch State Park   State
                                       Beach

N

0   20 mi

        50 km

SANTA   CAPITOLA
CRUZ

Map of Coastside State Parks. *Janet Taggart.*

I

McNEE RANCH STATE PARK

DUNCAN McNEE, SAVVY SPECULATOR

McNee Ranch is located on the west face of Montara Mountain, north of Half Moon Bay and south of Pacifica. Once the property of landowner Duncan McNee, the 525-acre site opened in 1984 as part of Montara State Park. Remnants of the Ocean Shore Railroad tracks and a World War II military bunker can still be seen. The ocean views are spectacular, and you may even have the extra benefit of seeing gray whales or humpback whales during their annual migrations.

LEAVING RENFREW

Duncan McNee was born in 1849 in Renfrew, Canada. Named after a city in Scotland, Renfrew means "point at the current." Appropriately, the small town rests along the banks of the picturesque Bonnechere River just west of Ottawa in eastern Ontario. Renfrew is reminiscent of Scotland's lush landscapes, rolling hills and long, flowing rivers, drawing Scottish immigrants for decades.

The community was settled largely due to logging. "The center of town then was what is known as an ash swale, a low wet spot of good land, timbered by ash, oak and balsams," a writer of the time revealed. "To the south of the town, there was the finest hardwood grove in the area with beech, black birch and big maples. Along the river bank, the forest was mostly evergreen, red pine, spruce and cedar."

Duncan McNee was born in Renfrew, Canada, in 1849. The town rests along the banks of the Bonnechere River west of Ottowa. *Earl Andrew.*

Renfrew's development was gradual. The first store was opened in 1840, followed by a gristmill. Eventually, the town boasted a blacksmith shop, tannery, cobbler, sawmill, carriage shop, brewery, post office, doctor's office, axe factory and tailor. There was no bridge across the Bonnechere in those days. If people needed to cross the river, they stood on the bank and yelled. The family that owned the farm at the crossing point would row over in a boat to ferry them across. Later, a wooden bridge was built, followed by a wire bridge in 1895.

Duncan was one of ten children. His parents, Duncan John McNee and Isabella Stewart McNee, were Scottish immigrants. They moved from Perth near the western coast of Scotland to improve opportunities for Duncan's father as a "general laborer." Duncan left Renfrew in 1864 at the age of thirteen, not knowing what his future would hold. Like so many others, he only knew that he was willing to work hard to make a better life for himself.

After making his way to San Francisco, he began working in the United States Land Office, created in 1858 to "protect and manage titles and claims of any lands" within state limits. By 1862, the State of California acquired interest in nearly nine million acres of land from the federal public domain within its boundaries for various purposes, including reclamation and the funding of public education. Managing this much property was a complicated task. Duncan loved the challenge and would rise to become chief clerk of the office.

Adept Transactions

Around 1870, Duncan met a man with whom he formed a partnership, Allexey W. Von Schmidt. Allexey left New York in 1849 to prospect for gold in California. "He heard about the gold at Sutter's Fort and came looking," a biographer wrote. "Trained as a civil engineer and surveyor, he departed the gold prospecting camps, to return to surveying."

Allexey worked on small and large projects throughout California, including in Contra Costa County, Rancho San Miguel, Yuba County, Mono Lake and Yosemite. As his reputation grew, the City of San Francisco took notice and hired him. One of the large projects was to help build the city's first dam and drinking-water aqueduct system. He also became a key engineer in San Francisco, working on the famous cable car system.

Duncan and Allexey were ambitious, determined, energetic problem solvers. They both believed that "anything is possible." Together, they forged a creative, successful dredging business in San Francisco. Dredging is the removal of sediments and debris from the bottom of lakes, rivers, harbors and other water bodies. It is a routine necessity in waterways around the world because sedimentation, the natural process of sand and silt washing downstream, gradually fills channels and harbors.

The central idea of dredging is maintaining or increasing the depth of navigation channels, anchorages and berthing areas to ensure the safe passage of boats and ships. Vessels require a certain amount of water in order to float and not touch the bottom of the body of water. This water depth continues to increase over time as larger and larger ships are utilized.

The duo's enterprise focused on dredging harbors, rivers, creeks and canals. Their projects included widening channels in San Francisco Bay, making improvements at Oakland Harbor and dredging the Navy Yard at Mare Island. They employed Allexey's patented dredge, boasting, "This is the only dredge that conveys excavated material ashore through hydraulic conduits in one operation, as fast as taken and as far distant as may be deemed."

Over time, Duncan became adept at both business and property transactions. His experience in the U.S. Land Office and the consequent intimate knowledge as to the most desirable tracts held by the government enabled him to invest his earnings wisely. He invested money from his successful dredging company in mines, oil fields and timberlands all over the West. He owned eight hundred thousand acres of land in every county of California as well as the mineral rights for fourteen thousand acres in

In the 1880s, Duncan McNee forged a partnership with Allexey W. Von Schmidt. Their company dredged harbors, rivers, creeks and canals. *Sierra College.*

nineteen counties. McNee Ranch was a small part of Duncan's empire. His ranch's valley was the site of cattle grazing. On its slopes, hay and grain were grown and harvested. Years later, the ranch was used a dairy farm.

Duncan passed away in 1913 while visiting one of his sons, Royal, in Santa Rosa, located about fifty miles north of San Francisco. "With him when the end came were the members of his family, his wife and daughter having been summoned home from the east where they were tarrying after a European trip," an obituary noted. "He is survived by his wife, Mrs. Hattie McNee, a daughter, Miss Claire McNee, and two sons, Albert E. and Royal J.H. McNee."

Duncan's firm, McNee Company, endured beyond his death, with the last holdings being sold in 1964. The State of California purchased the 625-acre ranch in the late 1970s and officially opened it in 1984 as part of Montara State Park.

"REACHES THE BEACHES"

Atop Montara Mountain, and within the boundaries of McNee Ranch State Park, remnants of the Ocean Shore Railroad as well as an abandoned World War II military bunker can still be seen. Montara Mountain was originally known by the name *Montoro*. The word is thought to be a misspelling of several Spanish words that describe mountains and forests, such as montuoso, montaraz, montaña and montosa, meaning "valley of brush" or "wooded valley." It was designated as Montara Mountain when somebody misread a map.

Visitors to the area are treated to sweeping vistas of the Pacific Ocean and the San Mateo coast. "Poets have described Montara Mountain as brooding and as a gray-green granite hulk," one writer mused. "The mountain is also sunshine and shadow and unforgettable fragrances. It is a place where land and sea meet like no place else on earth."

The mountain is situated along the ocean bluffs of Highway 1. It's the same setting where passengers in Ocean Shore Railroad trains sat awestruck by the wondrous views. Established in 1905, the railroad blasted through the ridge for its roadbed, referring to the resulting notch as the "Saddle Cut." Later, most of the Ocean Shore right-of-way was paved over and turned into Highway 1.

The railroad started with $3 million in capital from a group of investors in San Francisco. J. Downey Harvey, a popular and magnetic businessman with roots in Southern California, was the railroad's first president. Coffee king James A. Folger was vice-president. According to one observer, "they saw the coastal beauty of the Pacific Ocean as a perfect 'picnic route' for well-to-do city folk interested in a beach day trip. Also, the idea of a new train line excited Coastside residents, who were accustomed to traveling for hours by stagecoach to get to more populated areas such as San Francisco."

The railroad's trademark catchphrase was "Reaches the Beaches." Energetic promoters pointed out, "Where else could anyone leave the tension and turmoil of a great city like San Francisco and find peace and tranquility within an hour? The serious fisherman will find streams teeming with trout. The soul searcher will find wooded glens and secluded beaches."

The railroad's route started in San Francisco and ran along a coastal path through the small villages that later became Pacifica, Montara, Moss Beach, El Granada and Half Moon Bay. The tracks ended at Tunitas Creek, south of Half Moon Bay. Initially, trains were intended to run as far as Santa Cruz, but the roadbed was never completed.

Within a few years, the increasing use of automobiles and trucks, as well as the commitment of taxpayer dollars to build roads, sounded the death knell for the Ocean Shore Railroad," one historian explained. "The train

Montara Mountain is part of McNee Ranch. It's the same setting where Ocean Shore Railroad trains hugged the coastline between 1905 and 1920. *Author's collection.*

tracks constantly developed problems from the eroding sand and dirt. When road crews couldn't keep the tracks open during winter storms, travelers took to their Fords and farmers loaded their produce onto trucks."

Plagued by troubles, including financial woes and the 1906 earthquake, the last scheduled Ocean Shore train ran on August 16, 1920. Several of the depots still exist, albeit in varying forms. Most have been remodeled as residences, restaurants and even a day-care facility. But the memories linger on. Many families have passed on stories of riding the Ocean Shore Railroad, recalling the "long reverberating whistle" of a bygone age.

REMNANTS OF WORLD WAR II

During World War II, McNee Ranch was commandeered by the U.S. Army. It built a bunker on Montara Mountain and used isolated sections of the ranch as a commando training site. Coastsiders of the time reported being ordered off the slopes surrounding the ranch.

The bunker was the centerpiece of a military reservation and one of five "fire control stations" built by the army between Pacifica and Half Moon Bay. Men in these stations kept watch for attacking Japanese ships. Their job was to telephone the enemy's coordinates to massive gun batteries in the Marin Headlands and at Fort Funston in San Francisco.

These ten-foot-by-ten-foot rooms were manned by lookouts equipped with binoculars. Their job was to triangulate coordinates of approaching enemy ships. The coordinates were then sent by radio to artillery batteries, which used them to take aim at the vessels. "Our responsibility was to identify and report by telephone or radio on the movement of all ships and aircraft," one lookout explained. "There was the possibility that the enemy might attempt a landing and a stronger possibility that they would attempt to land saboteurs."

Just a few miles down the coast, the army also built an outpost with a radar tower and anti-aircraft machine guns along Pillar Point Bluff. A firing line with the various anti-aircraft guns and machine guns was laid out facing the ocean, allowing an open field of fire. Thousands of recruits trained, shot live rounds at targets off the coast and practiced beach landings. A Coast Guard seaman named Potter was a gunnery instructor at the school. "Sometimes, the trainees would get bored with practice and try to hit the planes pulling their targets," he said. "Later, radio controlled miniature planes were used."

A special squadron of Women's Air Service Pilots (WASPs) was stationed at the airstrip. They piloted tiny, one-person PQ-14 aircraft along the beach,

During World War II, McNee Ranch was commandeered by the U.S. Army. A bunker was built on Montara Mountain to watch for enemy ships. *Life magazine.*

towing targets for trainee anti-aircraft gunners to practice shooting. Their assignments were "hush-hush," and few knew that WASPs were flying from a mile-long airstrip in Half Moon Bay. "The duty was extremely dangerous," pilot Shirley Thackara acknowledged. "If the gunners missed the target, stray bullets could do damage to both civilians and pilots."

These measures were part of a sprawling defensive system the U.S. Army began constructing in the 1930s around the mouth of the Golden Gate. The work took on new urgency in 1941 after the Japanese bombed Pearl Harbor. The bunkers and other structures have been abandoned since 1949, when modern aircraft defenses removed the threats once posed by battleships.

The old military bunker atop Montara Mountain was once hidden in a nest of rock. Today, exposure to saltwater spray and ocean winds have significantly eroded the bluff and rusted the metal-and-concrete fortification. The remnants of the bunker resemble a mysterious relic. Even so, it remains a haunting symbol of an unforgettable era.

GRAY WHALE COVE

State park docents lead scheduled two-hour hikes from Gray Whale Cove, an adjoining state beach, to McNee Ranch. Although the trail is narrow and rough in some places, it hugs the western side of Montara Mountain, allowing spectacular views of the ocean below and perhaps a glimpse of whales. There are plants along the edges of the path that could do you harm, including poison oak and stinging nettles, so it is best to stay on the trail. Even when poison oak has no leaves, it can still cause a rash. Other, more pleasing plants that might be seen include coyote brush, coffee berry, California aster and Douglas iris. Signs of wildlife may also appear along the trail. There might be deer, coyotes and mountain lions. However, visitors are more likely to see tracks of wildlife rather than the critters themselves.

Gray Whale Cove was first known as "Match Box Cove" for early residents who lined the walls of their house with matchbook covers. In the 1960s, the name was changed to Gray Whale Cove to honor the migrating cetaceans that passed by.

Gray whales and humpback whales migrate annually along the coast. Gray whales are the species seen most often in Northern California. Their journey is one of the longest mammal migrations on earth. Their migration starts in the feeding grounds of the Arctic Ocean and ends ten thousand to twelve thousand miles south off the coast of Mexico to breed and calve in the warmer waters.

From the Arctic, the whales pass the Northern California coast from December through February. The mothers and calves return north between March and May. During their northward journey, the mothers stay closer to shore to protect the calves from predatory Orcas. This makes for easy viewing from the trail.

Gray whales can reach forty to fifty feet in length and weigh more than seventy-two thousand pounds when fully grown. They are dark gray in color with blotchy white patches. The white patches are variations in pigmentation, scars and even barnacles.

Humpback whales are almost black in color, with white markings along their underside, fins and flukes (tail). Their flukes are wide with an uneven end, and their pectoral fins are almost one-third of their body. They can reach lengths of fifty to fifty-five feet and weigh fifty-five thousand to sixty-six thousand pounds. They migrate from their winter calving and mating areas off Mexico to their summer and fall feeding areas off coastal California and can be seen from late April to early December.

Gray whales and humpbacks are called baleen whales, because they have no teeth. Instead, they have filter-feeding plates called baleen. While they were once hunted primarily for their oil, baleen or whalebone was also taken from the whales. Baleen is flexible and can be used for many products. Today, these magnificent mammals are protected, and we have the pleasure of watching them pass our coast, playing and nurturing their young.

2

BURLEIGH H. MURRAY RANCH STATE PARK

ROBERT P. MILLS, UNCONVENTIONAL LAND BARON

In 1857, Robert P. Mills purchased a homestead in Half Moon Bay. It later became the basis of Burleigh H. Murray Ranch State Park. Established in 1979, the 1,315-acre park was named after his step-grandson. A unique structure on the property is the only known example of an English-style bank barn in the state.

LEAVING "COTTONOPOLIS"

Born in Manchester, England, in 1823, Robert P. Mills was one of eight children. Manchester developed as a distribution center for raw cotton and spun yarn as well as a marketplace for products of a growing textile industry. Because of its dominance in the textile industry throughout the nineteenth century, the city became known as "Cottonopolis." The mills paid relatively high wages and employed large numbers of children. It's likely that when he was old enough, Robert worked in one of the mills.

Even as a lad, Robert knew that he was destined for something beyond the shores of his home. Described as "fair-haired and blue eyed," he boarded a ship for America in 1852, wondering what he might find, what he might do, what he might become. For a time, he subsisted by toiling in the California gold fields.

"The young man's enthusiasm overshadowed the fact that only the lucky few could realize success. Like most, Mills sought the elusive ore,

Robert P. Mills was born in Manchester, England, in 1823. Because of its textile industry, the city was known as "Cottonopolis." *McConnel & Company.*

only to eventually give up," a biographer remarked. "Unlike most, he did not return to his home and family but drifted into San Francisco, to survive by learning a trade."

He moved to San Francisco in 1856, working as a painter and a maker of windows before finding his calling as a manufacturer of ornamental glass. As a glazier, he designed and built ornamental stained-glass windows for churches and mansions. "He made and sold everything from globe lamps to intricate stained glass windows," one historian revealed. "He was highly regarded and was chosen to provide the ornamental glasswork for William Ralston's Palace Hotel.

With the rapid development of San Francisco, Robert had no problem finding work, and he invested his earnings wisely in local real estate. By 1865, Robert Mills was one of the richest men in San Mateo County. Although he never lived on the Coastside, he financed many of the early immigrant families that did. He owned a ranch near San Gregorio, large parcels adjacent to dairies in the Pilarcitos Valley and two lots in Spanishtown (later Half Moon Bay).

Some referred to Robert as the "Patron of the Coastside." According to one source, "He was well-known to Coastsiders and held several dozen promissory notes secured by professional mortgage agreements with Coastside residents who bought farmland or town property."

Mills Ranch

In 1889, Robert built a house, barn and other outbuildings on a parcel of land in Half Moon Bay. This working ranch was home to a succession of immigrant English, Irish, Italian and Portuguese tenant families. The original Victorian-style house burned around 1930 and was replaced by a smaller, ranch-style house. Ranch hands slept and ate in a small house east of the barn.

The Mills Barn, listed in the National Register of Historic Places, is a two-story dairy barn built with local fir and redwood. Since it is set into a hillside, the structure is called a "bank barn." George R. Borden, a noteworthy Coastside pioneer, appears to have been leasing the ranch during the barn's creation. Lumber from his prosperous timber mill is said to have been used in its construction.

Originally, it was two hundred feet long and could house one hundred dairy cows. It is California's only known example of an English-style bank barn. This unique formation allows farmers to drive loads up ramps to the second floor. Hay can be easily loaded into the hayloft and dropped through floor hatches to the animals below.

As part of the barn, a stone wall with evenly spaced buttresses once created animal stalls within the structure. Also on the property is a covered stone culvert that channeled the flow of drainage. An arched stone bridge made only with mortar and rock allowed for the passage of fully loaded wagons. A local newspaper declared, "The stone bridge will last for at least half a century, though under its arch flows a constant stream of water which in winter time is swelled to a raging torrent. It was built for a cost of about $300. The work is the only example of its type on the coast."

All of the stonework was the creation of an Italian stonemason, Guiseppi, or perhaps Giambatiste, B. Martini. Some called him Mike Bacheca DiMartini. But the name he most likely used was G.B. DeMartini. Under this moniker, he advertised his craft as "plastering, whitewashing, chimney building and bricklaying."

The ranch had a variety of buildings that supported dairy operations. Dairies in the late 1800s and early 1900s had no way to keep milk cold during shipment to markets like San Francisco. Instead, they made cheese that would keep for long periods and was easy to transport. There was also a blacksmith shop to keep horses shod and to repair farm equipment. Seeds and grain were stored on the first floor of the granary, while vegetables and meat were stowed in the cellar.

California's only example of an English-style "bank barn" is located at Burleigh H. Murray Ranch State Park. It was built in 1889. *California State Parks.*

Mills Ranch is located in a protected and somewhat isolated valley a few miles from the center of Half Moon Bay. The developed portion of the property sits in a relatively flat area, with Mills Creek flowing through the middle, dotted by eucalyptus trees and ringed by hills on all sides. Over the years, the ranch was described as "very productive and a beautiful place" by many of the tenants who leased the land.

Unconventional Personal Life

Robert's personal life was unconventional, to say the least. On the overland trip to California from the East Coast in 1856, he met an English couple, Rowland and Diana Chatham. After spending time together in the gold fields, the trio moved to San Francisco, living in separate residences. Robert and Rowland became business associates.

During the early 1860s, Robert began carrying on a romance with Diana. She ceased to share the same bedroom with her husband, and in 1863, the trio agreed that Robert should come to live with them. Robert and Diana shared a bedroom together while Rowland occupied a room next door. According to one writer, they all "remained friendly and sat together at the family dining table to eat."

With the money he accumulated as a glazier, Robert bought a lot in San Francisco and built a small home. Although he was spending most of his time with Diana and Rowland, he listed his house in San Francisco as his official residence. Robert also started seeking out other real estate investments. He purchased property on the Coastside as well as land on the southern portion of the San Francisco peninsula in Belmont.

In 1865, he rented a room at the Belmont Hotel in order to expand the villa of William Chapman Ralston. William, a banker, was known as the "silver king" of San Francisco. With riches gained from the Nevada Comstock Lode, he became one of the wealthiest and most powerful men in California. He founded the Bank of California and took a deep interest in the building of railroads and the establishing of woolen mills, sugar refineries, silk factories and steamship lines.

Robert's union with Diana produced a son, Robert Shofield, known as Bobby, and a daughter, Maria. The children kept Chatham as their last name. In the 1870s, he assumed a father's responsibility, allowing Diana to keep rents from his San Francisco properties so that she gained about $600 a month for their children's care.

Robert parted from his relationship with Diana around 1875. But Rowland's unexpected death from injuries sustained from a fall in 1885 changed the family dynamics yet again. At Diana's insistence, she and the children moved to Belmont to live with Robert.

"Spanish Town South"

In early 1890, Robert and three colleagues, the experienced dairymen Frank Madonna and Giulio Franciola and local merchant Joseph Debenedetti, organized a land development to be called Spanish Town South. As the principal financier, Robert used his considerable political associations to move the fifty-four-acre subdivision successfully through bureaucratic channels. Of twenty-one lots in the new tract, ranging from one- to five-acre parcels south of town along Main Street, all but one were sold in the first year.

That Robert loaned money to at least ten of the purchasers of Spanish Town South lots was no secret. In 1893, he continued to improve his dairy property and barn and became a partner in the first Coastside creamery. The *Redwood City Democrat* began referring to Spanish Town South as "Millsville." It reported: "South Spanishtown, Millsville, is growing rapidly. It is fast becoming a prominent place. Soon its parent will be its suburb."

Robert's commitment to and encouragement of the growth of the Coastside town paid off—for himself, for his partners and for the working-

A stone wall, created by an Italian stonemason, was built on Robert P. Mills' land. Much of it still stands. *Coastside State Parks Association.*

class immigrant population of which he had been part. Dairymen Madonna and Franciola introduced methods of sanitation and productivity in their operations, enhancing acceptance of their dairy goods. Soon, their products became San Mateo County's leading cash export.

The success of the Spanish Town South subdivision also brought much-needed community services, including the town's first newspaper, the *Coast Advocate* (in 1890), two creameries (1893 and 1895), electricity (1893), the county's first steel-reinforced concrete bridge over Pilarcitos Creek (1900) and the Sunset Telephone Company's establishment of service with San Francisco (1897).

"Although his efforts may be regarded by some as enlightened self-interest, there can be no doubt that Robert P. Mills and his many Coastside enterprises contributed materially to the development of Half Moon Bay," Kathryn Gualtieri, California's former State Historic Preservation Officer, reflected. "While the Spanish Town South tract may serve today as an abstract reminder of Robert Mills's Coastside commitment, surely the magnificent dairy barn he had constructed on his first Half Moon Bay property is the most appropriate reminder of his many contributions to the economic success of the community. No other buildings associated with Mills still stand."

A MARRIAGE AT LAST

In 1889, a Belmont neighbor who lost her husband three years prior garnered Robert's interest. Miranda Murray was known for her "social status, business acumen, strong-willed independence, fire and ambition." At last, he had found the woman he longed to marry. Unceremoniously, Robert sent Diana to San Francisco to live permanently.

Robert, now age sixty-seven, and Miranda, fifty-eight, were married on August 2, 1890. With her came her twenty-five-year old son, Burleigh Chase Murray, and her nineteen-year old daughter, Carrie, from her previous marriage to Lemuel Murray. Although they lived in Robert's home in Belmont, the couple also spent a good deal of time in Half Moon Bay, where Robert continued to buy and sell property.

Although Miranda did not allow Robert's illegitimate children to visit, he found time to see his son Bobby. Robert was proud of Bobby's career progress, from laborer to glazier to millworker and to sewing machine salesman.

When Robert passed away unexpectedly in 1897 of bronchitis, Miranda requested that no funeral or memorial service be held. For a time, she refused to see visitors. Robert was buried at Cypress Lawn in Colma. Since he did not leave a will, Miranda was appointed to administer his estate. At the time, the estate was valued at about $200,000, almost $7 million today.

MORE CONTROVERSY

Bobby and Maria Chatham filed a petition in court for two-thirds of their father's estate. Two years later, the estate trial began in San Mateo. The case dragged on for three weeks, called over fifty witnesses and became a full-blown media event. Diana Chatham was the most significant witness, clearly tracing the intimate details of her relationship with Robert.

Miranda startled the courtroom by producing a special piece of documentation. It was a journal, written in Robert's own hand, in which he acknowledged that he "had but one wife, no children and would leave no will." Unfortunately, the journal failed to impress the jury, which rendered a verdict in favor of Bobby and Maria.

Miranda appealed the decision to the California Supreme Court in January 1900. Two years later, the court reversed the decision and remanded it to a lower court for retrial. In April 1903, Bobby and Maria agreed to a settlement of about $15,000. Neither Bobby nor Maria appeared in court to argue further, and Miranda obtained primary control over the estate.

The controversy and publicity provided an opportunity for Bobby to run for sheriff of San Mateo County. Although he won the race, he did not stand for the position again when his term expired in 1908. He moved to Mendocino, where he bought a sheep-and-cattle ranch.

Miranda died of heart failure in 1919 at the Belmont estate where she had lived with Robert. She requested to be buried by her first husband, Lemuel Murray, in the family plot at Cypress Lawn in Colma.

Her tombstone reads simply, "Miranda E. Murray."

Miranda's son, Burleigh Chase Murray, took over management of the Mills Ranch. "Mr. Murray has devoted himself closely to the operation of the place, in which he has been very successful, and is now numbered among the solid and substantial farmers of his section of the county," a biographer wrote. "A man of industrious habits and sterling character, he commands the respect of his fellow men."

After he passed away in 1937, his son Burleigh Hall Murray inherited the property. When he died in 1978, his estate donated Mills Ranch the following year to California State Parks. Thankfully, we can visit the 1,300-acre ranch, hidden in a pristine valley south of Half Moon Bay.

The area offers solitude, bridged streams and a rich assortment of wildlife. It is home to bobcats, mountain lions, rabbits, coyotes, pack rats, mule deer, western fence lizards, California quail, owls and songbirds. Plants abound as well, including red currant, milkmaid, bleeding heart, trillium, salmonberry, twinberry, dogwood, wild cucumber and cow parsnip. The hill mass is covered with mature eucalyptus trees planted by Robert Mills when the barn was erected.

After shifting on its foundation, the unusual barn was shored up with posts and external bracing that run the length of the building. While the structure is still very visible, the interior is closed to the public for safety reasons. The barn was added to the National Register of Historic Places in 1900, one hundred years after its construction.

3

FRANCIS BEACH

MANUEL FRANCIS, DUTIFUL BROTHER

F rancis Beach is part of Half Moon Bay State Beach, which was established in 1956. The beach is associated with a historic shipwreck as well as an endangered species of shorebird. The area is named after rancher and merchant Manuel Francis. He and his brother Joseph were lifelong residents of the town and admired members of the local community.

PORTUGUESE IMMIGRANTS

The Azores is a cluster of fertile, volcanic islands about one thousand miles west of Portugal. Its climate is temperate and tropical, allowing lush plant life to thrive. There are waterfalls, craggy cliffs, farms, villages and churches—and, always, water everywhere.

Because of its natural setting in the Atlantic, the history of the islands is shaped by trade and travel. Discovered in the 1400s by explorer Gonçalo Velho Cabral, the Azores became a resupply station for ships returning from India spice runs on their way to Brazil and then from Brazil on their way back to mainland Portugal. Later, whaling became a key component of the economy, and the islands were a major port of call for American whaling ships.

Since the Azores was first inhabited, the main sources of survival and income were fishing and agriculture. Beginning in the 1830s, the area's economy faltered, and many people faced starvation. Potato rot and orange and grape fungus came, and drought occurred and recurred, further punishing a struggling population.

This short poem captures the feeling of the time: "The land is poor, the children swarm, our fields lack seed; our cradles fill, a double harm; God sends drought upon the farm and another mouth to feed."

Many people left the islands, seeking a better way of life. They had a persistence and determination to succeed, diligently saving money to buy their own land in America. Among the many immigrants who arrived in Spanishtown (later Half Moon Bay) in the 1860s were people from the Azores. Two of those immigrants were Joseph Machado and Antoinette Olivera. As was the custom of many Portuguese immigrants, they adopted a new American name, Francis.

MAKING A HOME IN HALF MOON BAY

Joseph, born in 1837, and Antoinette, born in 1842, married in 1858 and found their way from the Azores to Massachusetts. Facing poverty, a large number of immigrants fled from the Azores to New England. Men worked in textile mills, whaling and fishing. Women worked as seamstresses in garment shops. Joseph and Antoinette longed for a quieter way of life. They moved on to settle on a ranch in California's Spanishtown (later Half Moon Bay).

The region's earliest inhabitants were a tribe of Native Americans called the Chiguan. Known today as the Ohlone, they were documented in the area over 5,800 years ago. When Spanish missionaries arrived in the mid-1700s, the site was used by Mission Dolores in San Francisco to graze its large herds of cattle, horses and oxen. After land grants were given to Spanish soldiers and civil leaders in the 1840s, the area was carved into several huge parcels, each consisting of thousands of acres of prime coastland.

The southern portion, originally called San Benito and later called Spanishtown, developed as the first real town in San Mateo County. In 1874, the city was renamed Half Moon Bay after the concave shape of the coast that forms its western border. The northern portion grew more slowly, sprinkled mostly with farms and dairies.

Joseph and Antoinette relished the rural, agricultural community so similar to the Azores. They enjoyed living in semi-isolated conditions, feeling that it was easier to preserve their old customs and foods. Their native cuisine was a rich, hearty style of cooking. Most dishes focus on seafood, pork, spicy stews, rich dairy products and sweet desserts. They savored family life, raising eight children—four boys and four girls.

According to a local newspaper, "They were respectable and industrious farmers."

Joseph Marshall Francis and Manuel Francis, born in 1872 and 1875, respectively, were the youngest of the boys. As teenagers, the brothers enjoyed playing together in the Half Moon Bay Cornet Band. One of the largest festivals, and their favorite, was the annual Fourth of July parade. "At 10 a.m. sharp, the honorary president of the day led the parade, a grand civic procession that marched down Kelly Street," the local newspaper reported. "The Half Moon Bay Cornet Band played the *Star Spangled Banner, Our Flag is There* and an exciting number called *Red, White and Blue*. Trailing behind the band was a lovely Fourth of July float, drawn by a team of fine local horses."

Joseph and Manuel each became proprietors of their own businesses and prominent merchants. Joseph began his career as a clerk at Boitano's General Merchandise Store and Saloon. Opened in 1873 by Italian immigrant Giuseppe Boitano, the enterprise became one of the city's oldest continuous places of business. The downstairs portion of the two-story building housed the store and saloon, and the upstairs served as family living quarters.

Spurred by the hope of economic advancement, Joseph started his own general merchandise establishment. He became one of the most successful businessmen in the city. In 1901, he married Angelina Debenedetti. Later, he was one of the founders of the Bank of Half Moon Bay and began serving on the San Mateo County Board of Supervisors in 1909. In 1913, he built a Craftsman-style home in the center of town that still stands today. It was a popular style of the day, emphasizing "the beauty of simplicity and modesty in architecture."

In 1920, Joseph and Manuel broke ground on a two-story store built in a Spanish Colonial Revival style, highlighted with decorative ceramic and clay tiles along the roofline. Downstairs was a general merchandise store with a card room and pool hall in the rear. Upstairs were the family residences and a kitchen. Today, it exists as the Francis Building on Main Street. Only Manuel lived long enough to see it through completion.

Joseph passed away in October 1920. "He was big-hearted, kind and generous, beloved and admired by all who knew him," one newspaper declared. "He was a tireless leader. His charitable acts, done quietly and without ostentation, aided many people on the Coastside. His life was worthy of emulation by every young man."

Manuel grew up a little in the shadow of his ambitious older brother. However, he eagerly followed in his footsteps, gaining a reputation for hard work, thrift and diligence. Manuel opened a butcher shop in Pescadero and later joined Joseph in the Francis Brothers General Store in Half Moon Bay. He married Louise Avilla in 1898. When he joined the board of supervisors in 1924, he disposed of his Pescadero interests, devoting himself to his political work and to his Half Moon Bay venture.

Manuel passed away in 1956, knowing he was well loved. One newspaper recalled a special birthday party held for him in 1927. "A crowd of friends and family turned out, noting his work to secure roads on the coast," the story said. "They gave him many gifts, including a ring with an opal in the center."

HISTORIC SHIPWRECK

The Francis brothers, and most of the town, would have been witness to a historic shipwreck that occurred in 1898. The *New York* was one of the most infamous ships to ever sail. Originally named the *T.F. Oakes*, the vessel was part of a trio of large full-rigged iron ships built in the United States. Veteran seamen called it the "finest looking sailing ship" they had seen.

Sadly, it did not live up to all the high praise. The vessel proved a heavy, dull and slow sailor as well as an unlucky vessel. Its first voyage broke all records for the longest passage, a leisurely 195 days, from New York to San Francisco. Bound for China on its second voyage, the *T.F. Oakes* was caught in a typhoon and nearly wrecked.

For the next decade, the *T.F. Oakes* continued to plod the seas. A particularly disastrous passage from Hong Kong to New York occurred in 1896. On July 5, the *T.F. Oakes* cleared Hong Kong with a cargo of hides and skins and a complement of twenty-five crew, Captain Reed and his wife, Hannah. A week out of Hong Kong, the ship was caught in a succession of typhoons, which blew it five hundred miles off course to the northeast. Captain Reed changed the usual course around the Cape of Good Hope in South Africa and continued the journey sailing toward Cape Horn in South America. The new route was five to seven thousand miles farther.

The voyage took over eight months. During that time, Reed was partially paralyzed by a stroke and many of the weary crew fell ill with scurvy. The disease progressed rapidly, killing six men and disabling everyone but the second mate and Mrs. Reed. As conditions continued to worsen, the captain's wife took the helm and steered the ship safely to port.

While the *T.F. Oakes* was at sea, it was purchased by another company that changed its name to the *New York*. After an overhaul, the ship sailed from New York on May 18, 1897. Bound for Shanghai and then Hong

The iron sailing ship *New York* wrecked along the beach in 1898. Local residents claimed many souvenirs from the vessel. *San Mateo County History Museum.*

Kong, the ship made the trip without incident. On the return voyage to San Francisco, the vessel carried Captain Thomas Peabody; his wife, Clara; their eight-year-old daughter, Claire; twenty crew; and a rich cargo of coffee, dry goods, firecrackers, flour, garlic, green beans, hemp, peanut oil, pineapples, porcelains, rattan furniture, silk, spices, tapioca rice, tea, tobacco and wine.

Unhappily, the vessel's newfound good luck was fleeting. Leaving Hong Kong's harbor on January 14, 1898, the *New York* was plagued by unceasing storms. "From the first day we had a miserable time. Our ship ran into storm after storm," Claire Peabody wrote later.

About nine hundred miles off the California coast, the vessel ran into a furious squall, which snapped the main mast. Gales continued to batter the ship as it struggled up the coast. In the early morning hours of March 13, 1898, the *New York* became lost in heavy fog and was driven broadside onto the beach in Half Moon Bay. The misguided vessel missed its destination by a mere thirty miles.

Over the next few hours, the *New York* settled in the sand about two hundred yards from shore. Captain Peabody and his crew made preparations to launch the two undamaged lifeboats. Carrying the captain's wife and daughter and eight men, the first boat narrowly escaped destruction against the *New York*'s iron hull, filled with water from the crashing waves and nearly capsized. Scores of local residents who had dashed to the scene formed a human chain into the sea and snatched the helpless group from the undercurrent.

Over the next few days, the ill-fated *New York* sank deeper and deeper until it lay buried in twenty-three feet of sand. By March 16, the iron ship was filled water, the main hatch was broken, cabin windows were smashed, furniture was awash, the forecastle was completely gutted and the vessel had a decided list. "The tapioca rice in her hold had burst the deck and might force the hull apart," the *New York Maritime Register* reported. "The vessel had fallen over to starboard and the seas were breaking over her. Her back was broken."

Before the customs inspectors arrived to take possession of the cargo, local residents claimed many souvenirs from the ship. "My father, along with other young men, went out to claim relics," one woman confessed. "I have in my home the big arm chair taken from the captain's cabin."

Several boxes of hand-painted chinaware also disappeared, finding their way into Half Moon Bay homes. Some still survive in excellent condition. A local rancher took possession of the ship's bell. After tolling out so many hours at sea, it hung on the water tower of his ranch, where it was used to call the hands to their meals. Today, the bell is in the hands of a private collector.

ENDANGERED SHOREBIRDS

Francis Beach is the southernmost portion of four scenic areas comprising Half Moon Bay State Beach. Running northward from Francis Beach are Venice Beach, Dunes Beach and Roosevelt Beach. The protected shoreline stretches four miles. It is a fitting tribute to Manuel Francis and his family that Francis Beach is a nesting area for the western snowy plover. In the Azores, there are over four hundred species of birds, including several types of Plovers.

The little bird is six inches long and has light black, brown and white feathers with dark patches on either side of the neck, behind the eyes and on the forehead. They call to one another in a low-pitched "ku-wheet." They can be hard to spot as they scurry down to the water's edge for food. When

Francis Beach is a portion of four scenic areas that make up Half Moon Bay State Beach. It is named after dignitary Manuel Francis. *California State Parks.*

resting, they choose depressions in the sand, such as footprints, where they are camouflaged and out of the wind.

Prior to 1970, plovers numbered in the thousands and bred at fifty-three locations along the California coast. Today, it's estimated that approximately 2,300 western snowy plovers survive in twenty-eight breeding areas. This decline in population resulted in plovers being added in 1993 to the list of threatened species under the Endangered Species Act. The western snowy plover is the smallest of the nine species of North American plovers.

The coastal population breeds along the Pacific coast from southern Washington to southern Baja California, Mexico, with the majority of birds breeding along the California coast. Nesting season runs from mid-March through mid-September, coinciding with the season of greatest human recreational use.

Plovers feed and nest in open sand on the beach just above high tide lines, where human activity is the greatest. This leaves them vulnerable to human and predator activity alike. Nests, or scrapes, about the size of a footprint are lined with shells or pebbles, making them difficult to detect and easily crushed. In addition, the invasion of nonnative plants such as European beach grass creates a significant loss of habitat.

PLOVER PATROL

Usually, plovers lay a "clutch" or group of three buff-colored eggs spotted with black, making them perfectly camouflaged in the sand. This may take four to five days. Both parents take turns incubating the eggs, with the female

Francis Beach is a nesting area for the western snowy plover. The tiny bird is protected under the Endangered Species Act. *Audubon California.*

tending them during the day and the male taking over at night. On Francis Beach, the parents often switch places on the nest several times a day. The pattern of sharing incubation duties seems to be different for each pair.

If a predator approaches the nest, the plover jumps off the nest, crying for help and dragging one wing on the ground. The predator follows, thinking the bird is vulnerable. The plover flies a short distance along the sand and continues dragging its wing. This "broken wing" trick fools the predator, which soon wanders off in search of other prey.

The daily routine is challenging, even arduous, but with luck, in three to four weeks chicks begin pecking their way out of their shells. One by one, the baby birds emerge wet and wobbly from the cracked eggs. Chicks leave the nest within hours of hatching but cannot fly for a month.

Rather than relying on their parents, they are "visual foragers," using a run-stop-peck method of feeding. On spindly legs, the chicks scurry about, instinctively pecking, snatching and gobbling bugs and flies. When they are ready to fly, fledglings are often so awkward that they flap and bounce several miles along the beach trying out their new wings. Their life span will be about three years, but some live up to fifteen years.

To help ensure their survival, Francis Beach sponsors a Plover Patrol program. Volunteers are on the beach during nesting season to spot nests and help build enclosures around them to protect the eggs. They also study and collect data about the plovers and educate the public about these precious tiny birds. Plovers are, indeed, a state treasure.

4

POMPONIO STATE BEACH

POMPONIO, FREEDOM FIGHTER

Often overlooked by Coastside visitors is Pomponio State Beach in San Gregorio, located about twenty minutes south of Half Moon Bay. Established in 1960, major features of the site are rugged caves that have been carved into the cliffs by roaring wind and waves. The cove celebrates the rich history of the evocative Native American Pomponio, who once hid in the caves. Taken into the Spanish mission system as a child, he fought for his freedom after years of oppression.

Meeting the Miwoks

In 1579, Sir Francis Drake was exploring the West Coast in search of the elusive "northwest passage." The ship's chaplain, Francis Fletcher, and others kept journals of that voyage. In June, Drake and his crew anchored near San Francisco Bay for five weeks to prepare for the long sail across the Pacific Ocean. There they met the native inhabitants, the Coast Miwok.

"After our coming to anchor, the people of the country showed themselves, sending off a man to us in a canoe. He spoke to us continually as he came rowing on," a book based on the voyage's journals explains. "He used many gestures and signs, moving his hands, turning his head and body many ways. After his oration ended, with a great show of reverence and submission, he returned back to shore again."

Following several of these encounters, Drake landed his men with provision and tents. They were uncertain about the necessity of defending themselves. However, the Miwok were peaceful people, living by hunting, gathering and fishing. They were highly distinctive because of the tattoos and paint they used to adorn their bodies. Chaplain Fletcher with the Drake expedition wrote, "They are of a free and loving nature, without guile or treachery."

Miwok food included a staple diet of acorns, which they ground into meal and stored for up to a year. The meal was used to make soup, cakes and bread. They collected other nourishment such as buckeye nuts, mushrooms, various greens, roots, bulbs and berries. They hunted deer, black bear, elk, fowl and small game such as jackrabbits and quail. Fish was another important Miwok food source, particularly salmon, but also included trout and shellfish.

During the summer, the semi-nomadic Miwok lived in temporary pointed, conical cedar bark shelters. They were constructed using several poles tied together and covered with bark and sticks over the framework. Their more permanent winter homes consisted of villages of semi-subterranean winter dwellings built up to fifteen feet into the ground. The Miwok pit house was constructed of earth and brush with a pitched roof that was completely covered in earth. The winter houses had a central firepit and a smoke hole to allow smoke to escape and also let in light and air. Entrance was accessed by a ladder on top of the roof.

Although some Miwok were coastal people and others were inland people, they shared a similar social structure. "We had laws that told us how to live, how to marry, treat our children, continue our culture, care for the land, and respect the rights and property of others," a descendant noted. "We had our own government, our own territory, our own religion. We lived well in those conditions."

According to one historian, "With Drake's encounter, the Westernization of the native Miwoks began. They were able to continue living peacefully for two centuries, until the Spanish discovered San Francisco Bay in 1769. By 1776, Mission Dolores had been built and the subjugation of Miwoks as laborers and servants was in full sway."

MISSION SYSTEM

The first Spanish exploration by land occurred in 1769, when Gaspar de Portolá led an overland expedition from Baja (lower) California to Alta (upper) California. As other nations expressed increasing interest in Alta California, Spain sought to expand its influence in the area.

Spanish soldiers and missionaries were sent to establish permanent settlements in the form of missions. These missions represented the first major effort by Europeans to colonize the Pacific coast. In all, twenty-one were built, stretching 650 miles along the El Camino Real, a commemorative route from San Diego to Sonoma connecting the twenty-one missions along the coast of California. Each was placed where towns and trade could be readily developed.

The manner of Spanish settlement followed the same pattern at each mission. A cross was erected, Mass was celebrated and attempts were made to contact local tribes. Each mission needed Native labor to support itself and, later, to produce food, clothing and tallow for trade with nearby settlements and Yankee ships.

As the coast gradually opened to trade, word of the missions' growing herds of cattle drew ships eager to obtain hides and tallow in exchange for

Spanish soldiers and missionaries established permanent settlements in California called missions. They used Native American men, women and children as laborers. *California Missions Resource Center.*

commodities such as sugar, chocolate, tea and cloth. Customarily, mission priests traded directly with ship captains.

Initially, the Miwok and other Native Americans were drawn to missions by padres who reached out to them. According to Father Luis Antonio Martinez, "With the first buildings started or even before they were begun, the padres endeavored, by means of gifts and kind treatment, to attract the natives."

They were curious about Spanish religious practices, customs and skills. They came to participate in something new and form alliances with the powerful newcomers. At first, they were allowed to make occasional visits to their former surroundings and homes. Later, they were expected to stay at the missions, work hard and live in a prescribed manner.

According to one source, "The Franciscans established the missions with two primary goals: create an Indian work force capable of producing enough grain for the military and regulate the Indians' moral conduct and religious practices. The mission system's collateral damage was nearly total—the natives' food supplies were destroyed, their culture and beliefs were banned and their villages were decimated. Many smaller tribes disappeared altogether."

CRUMBLING WAY OF LIFE

Over time, dietary changes and disease took a toll on the Native American population. As more workers were needed, Spanish soldiers turned to sending raiding parties to capture people and force them into the missions.

The men labored as blacksmiths, brickmakers, candlemakers, carpenters, farmers, shoemakers, tanners and weavers. The women toiled at culling and grinding grain, sewing, sifting flour, spinning yarn and washing. Children performed chores in the garden or helped carry firewood.

Every moment of their time was planned, supervised and restricted. As a result, most of the California tribes living and working at the missions were dissatisfied. Strict discipline enforced by the missionaries caused unrest, even violence.

Mexico achieved independence in 1821, taking Alta California with it, but the missions maintained authority over laborers and kept control of vast landholdings. By the 1830s, California was a thinly settled territory that relied on missions for the bulk of its agricultural goods.

Although the missions were expected to become self-sufficient, they barely prospered. Relying mostly on raising cattle and crops, they struggled with soil depletion, inefficient fertilization and frequent droughts. Suffering from unfamiliar diets, sanitation problems and disease, mission workers tended to be malnourished, dispirited and often sick. Some ran away, many perished.

Further troubles developed in 1834, when the Mexican congress passed a new law ordering the secularization, or "disestablishment," of California's missions. Missionaries were replaced, and property promised to Native workers was sold to others. French immigrant Ernest de Massey observed, "The deserted huts of the Indians, who left the missions to resume their way of life, are falling to pieces."

POMPONIO REBELS

A legendary Coast Miwok who rebelled at the mission system was Jose Pomponio. Although his native name was Lupugeym, he was baptized and named after an obscure sixth-century bishop, Pomponius. Having been taken to San Francisco's Mission Dolores in 1803 at age four, he was raised there by his mother. His uncle worked as the mission's Miwok interpreter and witness at mission weddings from 1800 to 1805. However, by the time he was nine, most of Pomponio's family had died from illness. Eight years later, his entire extended family had passed away.

"He married an Indian girl, and, with her, lived in a little adobe house, a few paces from the mission church," one historian wrote. "Pomponio and Rosa lived the regular life of the neophytes, working at various occupations of the community—Pomponio tilling the ground and caring for the crops, and helping in the making of bricks for the houses; Rosa spinning and weaving and cooking. After they were married they continued with their customary labors, still under the tutelage of the padres."

By the time he was twenty-one, Pomponio began to feel unsettled, questioning the legitimacy of Spanish authority over his life. He gathered together a band of rebels known as "Los Insurgentes." They were not all Coast Miwok and included young men from the East Bay, San Diego, San Gabriel, Carmel and Soledad Missions. Their common language would have been Spanish.

"Pomponio was the cause of many wild nights in the settlement," one newspaper account disclosed. "Every so often, he broke from the watchful fathers and returned to his bloodthirsty comrades, mustering them into marauding bands that would swoop down in the dark upon the clusters of

Pomponio was baptized and raised at San Francisco's Mission Dolores. Taken there in 1803 by his mother, he rebelled at the mission system. *Robert Dawson.*

adobes that sought shelter in the shadow of Mission Dolores. They would ransack the dwellings and flee to the safety of their lair."

More often, they would creep stealthily into the settlement in the early morning hours and make away with the corralled horses. Pomponio and his band engaged in a lucrative trade in stolen mission horses. Mission-raised, the rebels did not inherit the ability to live off the land. As a result, they were reliant on their supporters at missions and their surrounding rancherias for sustenance and supplies.

Some offered to help out of fear that their crop reserves and horses would be stolen. Many of their supporters stood in solidarity against the mission system. They viewed the rebels as strong and fearless, having courage that they lacked to fight back. A few joined the rebels. The exact number of Pomponio's band is unknown. Some historians say there were as few as six or seven; others believe there were about twenty.

Pomponio was uniquely dangerous to the Spanish, because he was a product of the mission system. Unsurprisingly, the Spanish branded him an "unsavory character," a dangerous murderer, thief and rapist who preyed on other Indians as well as Spaniards. He was labeled "evil" by Father Juan Cabot of Mission Dolores in dispatches to Governor Pablo Vicente Solá. Solá was a Spanish officer and the twelfth and last Spanish colonial governor of Alta California. The padre claimed that Pomponio and his band were raiding rancherias in present-day Marin County and generally terrifying the local Spanish population.

While at large, Pomponio executed successful raids on a wide range of targets, including the San Francisco Mission and Presidio. He roamed across the entire San Francisco Bay area, establishing hideouts in numerous, secluded areas. Pomponio evaded officials for years, even escaping jail several times. In 1823, secret messages among priests, the governor and the comandante of the San Francisco Presidio revealed plans to capture Pomponio at one of his coastal cave hideouts in the remote Santa Cruz Mountains.

Subsequent letters reveal their disappointment in failing to find him. However, the soldiers left their calling card, a foreboding crucifix etched into the rock. A *Santa Clara News* article dated November 12, 1869, identified his cave as being near a waterfall in Devil's Canyon in what is now Long Ridge Open Space Preserve. This canyon is steep and dangerous, and there is no trail.

Eventually, Pomponio was captured. Accounts vary regarding his last days. The story of his final fate is just as elusive as he was in life. We do know that after several unsuccessful attempts, Spanish soldiers captured him in San Raphael in today's Marin County. He was near the mission named after Saint Raphael, the angel of bodily healing. It began as an asistencia, or helper, to Mission Dolores.

According to one story, "Four soldiers, armed with muskets, were upon him, one on each side, one in front and one in back. They were close to him before he was aware of their presence and escape was impossible. He was seized and his arms bound behind him almost as soon as he knew he was captured."

After Pomponio was captured by Spanish soldiers in 1824, he was taken to the Presidio of Monterey and executed by a firing squad. *Barrand Taylor.*

Pomponio was taken to the Presidio of Monterey, where he was clapped in chains in a tiny cell. The presidio, a military installation, was one of four presidios established by Spain in California. It consisted of a square of adobe buildings located near Lake El Estero in the vicinity of what is now downtown Monterey. Monterey was protected by a fort with eleven cannons and was the strongest of the presido fortresses.

Pomponio was tried by court-martial for murdering a soldier and sentenced to death on February 6, 1824. He was executed by a firing squad and buried secretly. Pomponio remained a hero to many long after, creating a legend that has lasted two centuries.

POMPONIO BEACH

What is now Pomponio State Beach was once a hideaway for Pomponio and his band of rebels. The site has some steep and very high coastal bluffs bordering the ocean. Much of the beach is difficult to access because of thick vegetated hillsides and steep sandstone cliffs. The beach is known as a pocket beach, a sandy expanse formed at the outlet of creeks and protected to the north and south by high cliffs. Sometimes, the remaining beach is strewn with captivating formations of driftwood. There are many sea caves, formed at the base of the cliffs by the erosion of waves.

The hidden reaches of this beach can be explored by walking at lower tides north or south below the picturesque promontories. Each route is a stunning beach walk ending at other state beaches, Pescadero State Beach to the south and San Gregorio State Beach to the north.

The major draw of Pomponio State Beach is enjoying the beautiful ocean setting. Birds of all types visit the area throughout the year. In winter, gull flocks can be present at the creek mouth. Other species include sea ducks, assorted shorebirds such as shearwaters and sandpipers as well as migrant raptors, hawks and falcons.

Here, we are reminded of the value of living in a world fully attuned to nature, the kind of world in which Native Americans once flourished. Here is a place that is fitting for a legend. We can easily imagine Pomponio slipping along the secluded coastal cliffs and caves at the beach that bears his name. A shadow here, a glimpse there; the powerful echo of a brave spirit aching to be free.

5

PEBBLE BEACH

LOREN COBURN, SCHEMING BUSINESSMAN

Pebble Beach is a part of Bean Hollow State Beach, established in 1958. This beautiful expanse of shoreline is composed of gleaming gemlike pebbles. The area once belonged to Loren Coburn, a controversial and unpopular businessman who wanted to build a resort and charge people for the pleasure of seeing the pebbles.

PANAMA FRENZY

Born into meager circumstances in 1826, Loren Coburn vowed to rise from destitution and make his mark on the world. After both of his parents passed away, he left his home in Vermont to live with older brothers in Massachusetts. "He was treated badly and the neglect had a profound effect on his desire to succeed," one historian explained. "He yearned to slip away and the California gold rush provided him with his opportunity. He absorbed the tales of striking it rich and was seduced by the promise of escaping poverty."

While in Massachusetts, Loren met and married Marie Antoinette Upton. They had one child, a boy named Wallace Loren Coburn, whom they fondly called Wally. In 1851, the Coburns shipped from New York on the steamer *Falcon*. Along with the *Ohio* and the *Georgia*, the *Falcon* was one of the first steamships to carry passengers to Panama.

The *Falcon*, built in 1848, weighed just under 900 tons and had a length of 244 feet and a width of 30 feet. It featured a wooden hull and side paddle

The U.S. Mail Steamship Company developed a line of ships that was a vital link between New York and Chagres, Panama. *Library of Congress.*

wheels. The builder was the noted New York shipbuilder William Henry Brown, best known for constructing the schooner yacht *America*, for which the America's Cup is named. Owned by the U.S. Mail Steamship Company, the *Falcon* carried U.S. mails from New York to California. Stops along the route included New Orleans, Havana and Chagres on the east coast of the Isthmus of Panama.

The Isthmus of Panama became a vital link, carrying passengers and mail between the eastern United States and California. The passage was a "short-cut" that reduced the voyage between New York and San Francisco to six thousand miles. Previously, the only route available was a lengthy fifteen-thousand-mile voyage around Cape Horn in South America. The Panama Canal, which would offer a waterway through the Isthmus of Panama, would not be completed until 1914.

Along with the Coburn family, thousands of prospectors sailed from Atlantic ports and made a fifty-mile journey across the isthmus by wagon, on mules and on foot along jungle trails. Reaching the Pacific, they then took another ship for California. Fares for the entire trip were between $330 and $400 in staterooms, $290 to $330 in lower cabins and $165 to $200 in steerage. Each person was allowed 250 pounds in personal baggage. Although the trip remained arduous and expensive, the Panama route became hugely popular. One traveler declared, "Speed was vital if the best gold claims in California were to be found."

Unfortunately, the small village of Chagres did not make a good impression on most passengers. Because of a sandbar, arriving vessels anchored about a mile from the landing place. Sometimes, when the seas were heavy, it was impossible to land. Steamers sat rolling off the mouth of the river for days before passengers could be put ashore.

Canoes called "bungos" carried people ashore across swirling, muddy water. The canoes, which were advanced by simple poles, could carry only two to four passengers at a time. Many travelers grumbled that the experience of crossing the isthmus was "like a nightmare." Even after weary wayfarers descended to the Pacific and Panama City, there were few ships to take them to California. Many were stuck in Panama City for weeks, even months. Then, each arriving vessel was mobbed with a mass of people fighting to get aboard.

After passing safely over the Isthmus of Panama, the Coburn family took passage on the ship *Panama*, arriving in San Francisco on June 1. From there, they went to the northern mines by way of Sacramento, remaining for several months. Laden with the fruits of a successful mining experience, they returned to San Francisco, where Loren established a livery business. Four years later, he sold the stable to purchase another, which remained active for twelve years.

Wave-Polished Stones

In 1862, Loren purchased Rancho Butano and Rancho Punto del Año Nuevo, which included the land at Pigeon Point. The two properties amounted to seventeen thousand prime acres along the San Mateo County coast. Part of the Año Nuevo property encompassed a cove known as Pebble Beach.

Filling the beach were small, lustrous stones "from the size of a grain of wheat to that of a good sized walnut." Their gemlike appearance was dazzling. Some pebbles were translucent, others were colorfully tinted, revealing every hue of the rainbow. For years, families enjoyed playing, picnicking and savoring this unique seaside wonder. They would spend hours hunting for the best pieces of agate, opal, jasper and carnelians polished by the waves to shiny perfection.

According to one writer, "The scene became ludicrous with folks in their finery sprawled on the piles of pebbles, their heads stuck in holes that they'd dug in their passionate search. It's said that these collections could be found in all the upper class houses in San Francisco and along the coast."

Local residents and tourists came to regard the beach as their own. It had always been the custom that travelers were allowed to cross privately owned land. However, in 1891, Loren closed the gate to the beach and gave notice that "the carrying away of colored stones would be regarded as highway robbery."

Originally, he rented the land to two farmers, who declined to renew their leases because they were annoyed by the traffic to and from Pebble Beach. Loren developed a new scheme for the property. He decided to construct a resort, including a two-story hotel that offered luxurious amenities such as hot and cold running water. Visitors would be carried to the beach on horses from his stable. Naturally, he planned to charge seventy-five cents per person.

"COBURN'S FOLLY"

Loren Coburn's actions deeply offended the community. In protest, a mob broke down the gate, assembled on the beach and burned him in effigy. The following morning, he dispatched men to barricade the gate. After it was torn down again, he sought a warrant for the arrest of the ringleader, Joseph Levy.

Joseph Levy was a formidable foe. He and his brother Fernand had fled their home in Alsace-Lorraine in 1869 to avoid the pending Franco-Prussian War. Alsace is a province sandwiched between France and Germany along the Rhine River. For centuries, the two countries argued over possession of this land. The young men wanted to avoid conscription into the military.

Their father, Leon, was a wealthy merchant. He steered his sons to San Francisco, where their mother, Julie, spent her early years. It was also the home of Raphael Weill, a family friend who had grown up in Alsace. Weill became famous as the founder of the White House Department Store, a huge establishment known for its French atmosphere.

Fernand and Joseph journeyed by ship to San Francisco, making contact with Weill soon after their arrival. While they stayed for a while in a French hotel, the "small-town" boys were not enamored of the city. Fernand, not quite twenty, went to work in a gold mine in El Dorado County near Sacramento but soon was clerking at a local store. Joseph, just sixteen, clerked in a frontier store in Round Valley in Mendocino County. In 1872, they decided to settle in Spanishtown (later Half Moon Bay).

The duo purchased a store from Charles E. Kelly and Richard L. Mattingly. They called their new enterprise Levy Brothers, which reportedly "stocked groceries of all variety, crackers and pickles by the barrel, beer in kegs or bottles, fencing material, stoves, tools, wheelbarrows and farm implements."

They also operated the post office and the Wells Fargo Express Agency. Routinely, the brothers offered to extend credit to their customers. One

Loren Coburn's Pebble Beach Hotel was called "Coburn's Folly." It was built near this beautiful beach. *Ingrid Holthuis.*

writer observed, "The brothers, having faith in everyone, were generous in extending credit and their faith in humanity paid off."

Joseph moved his family farther south to Pescadero. He had the innovative idea to offer door-to-door sales to the rural community. "He pioneered this inland market on horseback, leading one of two pack-saddled animals with merchandise for immediate sale," one historian noted. "For families on isolated farms and in small villages, it was something of an event to have merchandise displayed in their own homes."

With stores now in three communities, the Levy Brothers continued their entrepreneurial growth by opening cheese factories, a stagecoach line and a lumber mill. Their growing empire more than rivaled that of Loren Coburn. In addition, they treated people well and were rewarded with loyal customers.

"Levy's defense at the jury trial centered on the fact that people had traveled over the Pebble Beach's cow trail for over twenty years, conferring upon it the legal status of a public road," one report explained. "By locking the gate, Coburn had obstructed and denied the public's right to use the road. Levy contended that unlocking the gate amounted to appropriate legal action. Following a tense trial, the jury agreed."

For years, a bitter battle continued over access to Pebble Beach. Loren found himself in court repeatedly. Although he continued with plans to build the hotel, most people turned their backs, and it never opened to the public. Occasionally, Coburn's business associates would hold private parties there, but most rooms remained empty. Guests never stayed overnight, except for a watchman who was hired to protect the property from vandals.

The hotel became known as "Coburn's Folly." Progress was plagued with a variety of construction problems and ground to a halt after the 1906 earthquake. In the 1920s, the building burned down. Over seventeen thousand charred planks were removed from the site. Author Minot J. Savage captured the saga of the Pebble Beach Hotel when he wrote, "Yonder round a point of rock, in a quiet, sheltered cove, where storm ne'er breaks and sea ne'er comes, the tourists never rove."

COMPLICATED PRIVATE LIFE

Throughout all of the controversy, Marie Coburn stayed at her husband's side. Tragedy struck in 1868, when their only child became seriously afflicted. Seventeen-year-old Wally fell ill from typhoid fever and nearly died. Although he survived the fever, his mind was never the same.

"Wally needed help with dressing and eating. A leather apron was draped around him before he sat down at the kitchen table," June Morrall wrote. "He got fresh air on tightly supervised walks and could not be left alone. He was called 'the boy,' a nickname which best described his new mental state."

Marie was deeply affected by Wally's illness and frequently felt unwell. Coburn sent for Marie's sister, Sarah Satira Upton, to help manage the household and to care for Wally. When Marie passed away of cancer in 1896, Sarah continued to stay with the family. In 1910, she and Loren married in San Francisco. She was seventy-three and he was eighty-four. On November 14, 1918, he died of pneumonia during an influenza epidemic.

Sadly, Sarah Coburn was not to live out the rest of her life in peace. On June 4, 1919, just six months after Loren's death, she was found brutally murdered. The handyman discovered the body. He called Andy Stirling, the foreman for one of Coburn's business colleagues, who reached the authorities. "The first sight that greeted my eyes was the body of Mrs. Coburn lying partially robed on her bed. Her head was crushed and bleeding," Stirling told a reporter from the *San Francisco News*. "There was blood on the wall. There was no sign of a struggle."

Initially, Wally was suspected of the crime. However, a psychiatrist determined that "with the mind of a child, he could not have done so." Speculation about who was responsible for the bludgeoning ran rampant. Perhaps someone named in Sarah's will was eager for an early share of her estate. While the district attorney indicated that there was another suspect, an arrest was never made.

Pebble Beach Today

Today, the small, shiny pebbles at Pebble Beach still exist. The pebbles are quartz that has been chipped from an offshore reef, tumbled ashore, then wave-polished and rounded into beautifully hued small stones. Deposits of the varicolored, water-worn quartz are several feet deep and include the varieties agate, chalcedony, jasper, moonstones and sardonyx. Collecting the stones is no longer allowed.

Also along the beach are outcroppings of sandstone. The surface of many of the rocks has been weathered into a honeycomb-like surface known as

Pebble Beach was named for the gemlike pebbles in the sand. Honeycomb-like surfaces known as tafoni hold deposits of the varicolored stones. *Ingrid Holthuis.*

tafoni. As holes begin to form, small pebbles become trapped inside. Wave action rolling the stones erodes away the mudstone, siltstone and sandstone, but it's the soft sandstone that results in the most dramatic effects. The honeycomb weathering creates an intriguing moonscape effect.

A nature trail meanders south along the cliffs through a well-established native coastal strand plant community. Leather leaf fern, lizard tail, coast buckwheat, beach primrose and seaside daisy all thrive here. Visitors should be aware, though, that native poison oak also thrives along parts of the trail. Every so often, the trail dips down to the sand and tide pools. Anemones, crabs, small fish, sea urchins and other marine invertebrates hide in the many still pools.

A group of adult harbor seals and their pups regularly bask on some of the large rocks just offshore. Their large, dark eyes watch hikers with open curiosity and little apprehension. Birds like Brandt's cormorants and brown pelicans also use the rocks as a safe perch to dry their wings.

The colors and textures found at this scenic beach are nothing less than captivating. Every view is truly a work of art and a photographer's paradise. When visiting, please do your part to keep the beauty of this area intact for others to enjoy. Take only photos home with you—they are the best souvenirs.

6

BUTANO STATE PARK

JAMES McCORMICK, COASTAL LUMBERMAN

Too name *Butano* probably came from the Spanish term for a drinking cup made from a bull's horn. The park's history has been shaped by Native people, European explorers and settlers and loggers. But nothing is more closely tied to the history of Butano than lumber mills. A central figure was Irish immigrant and Pescadero entrepreneur James McCormick. Today, an area that was crowded with logging camps is filled with the wonders of nature.

IRISH POTATO FAMINE

Ireland in the mid-1800s was an agricultural nation, populated by eight million inhabitants who were among the poorest people in the Western world. Only about a quarter of the population could read and write. Life expectancy was short, about forty years. The Irish married quite young and tended to have large families, although infant mortality was also high.

A survey in 1835 found half of the rural families in Ireland living in single-room, windowless mud cabins that didn't have chimneys. The people lived in small communal clusters, known as clachans, spread out in the beautiful countryside. Up to a dozen individuals lived inside a cabin, sleeping in straw on the bare ground, sharing the place with the family's pig and chickens.

The potato had become the staple crop in the poorest regions. More than three million Irish peasants subsisted solely on the vegetable, which is rich

During the Irish Potato Famine in the 1840s, thousands of people fled to America. Many perished on overcrowded "coffin ships." *The Alameda Sun.*

in protein, carbohydrates, minerals and vitamins such as riboflavin, niacin and vitamin C. It's possible to stay healthy on a diet of potatoes alone. The Irish often drank a little buttermilk with their meal and sometimes used salt, cabbage and fish as seasoning. Irish peasants were actually healthier than peasants in England and other parts of Europe, where bread, far less nutritious, was the staple food. Beginning in September 1845, the potato famine killed over a million men, women and children in Ireland and caused another million to flee the country.

The famine began quite mysteriously, with leaves on potato plants suddenly turning black and curly, then rotting, seemingly the result of the fog that wafted across the fields of Ireland. The cause was actually an airborne fungus originally transported in the holds of ships traveling from North America to England. Hordes of Irish individuals and families fled to America. Most departed from Cobh (pronounced "Cove" and then called Queenstown) in southern Ireland, making it the single most important port of emigration. They boarded ships bound for Boston, New York and Philadelphia.

Each "coffin ship" carried hundreds of emigrants. They were crammed with three others into a six-foot-square berth—"less room than in a coffin."

The berths were stacked three high in the holds of sailing ships that took five to seven weeks to cross the Atlantic. Some ships carried 1,200 steerage passengers, who were seldom allowed on deck. Faced with crowded and disease-ridden conditions, with poor access to food and water, thousands of people perished as they crossed the Atlantic.

New Life in a New Land

Peter and Catherine Gibeny McCormick were among those who left their home in Cobh in the 1840s. With them were two young sons, James and John. Once safely in America, the family settled in Carthage, New York. The tiny village sat along the Black River, where many industries developed. They included a blast furnace for making iron and small iron implements, a number of wood-based factories, an assortment of manufacturing plants and a tannery.

While the town was to the liking of Peter and Catherine, James and his brother longed for more. They left home for the West Coast, crossing the Isthmus of Panama and arriving in San Francisco on January 15, 1864. In a short time, the brothers settled in Santa Cruz. After about nine months, they relocated to Pescadero, where they would spend the rest of their lives.

During the early years, the brothers ranched, leasing the Mattei Ranch (also known as Willowside Farm) on Stage Road about a mile north of Pescadero. They also found time to marry. John wed Mary Eliza Ann Brownell, raising a large Irish family. James married Julia Shaffery, and they raised seven children—six daughters, Alice, Frances, Ella, Florence, Lillian and Julia and one son, James. To house his growing family, he built the well-known McCormick House on Stage Road near Pescadero Creek in 1873, now a cozy bed-and-breakfast.

"Pescadero is one of the most substantially built little villages in the state," one writer noted. "It is nestled cozily in a little valley and is surrounded by protecting hills which ward off a portion of the disagreeable fogs that frequently visit."

James launched a mercantile business and soon bought the Levy Brothers store, renaming it McCormick and Son. In addition, he rented a small building across the street from the store and opened a saloon called the Elk Horn. This is where the post office is today. Over time, he bought and managed more than one successful hotel and livery stable. In addition, he purchased 320 acres along Butano Creek; it is the Butano Canyon we know today.

Irish immigrant James McCormick settled in Pescadero in the 1860s. He launched numerous successful businesses in the small town. *California State Parks*.

According to one biographer, "The business interests of the little town of Pescadero are largely represented by the interests of James McCormick. Although not a native Californian, he has thrown himself heartily into the up-building of his adopted land, which owes much to his earnest efforts."

LOGGING SAGAS

In the 1880s, James established a logging mill in Butano with his friend James A. Hamilton. "The men who pioneered lumber mills were an unusual breed. They constantly battled against great odds," one historian pointed out. "Besides the deep, narrow canyon walls which presented an incredible challenge to the best of woodchoppers, these lumbermen faced the daily threat of such natural disasters as floods and raging fires."

The trees were primarily redwood, which is soft, resistant to rot and insects and easy to work with. They were selected for felling based on their accessibility and straight grain. "To be nearby when a big tree comes down is like being in an earthquake," one writer noted. "There is a whoosh sound, and then a thump, and then an after-tremor. Then you have absolute quiet and the absolute quiet is deafening."

Once trees were down, they were stripped of branches and bark and cut into relatively short lengths, usually about sixteen feet. This was done by men known as barkers or peelers. The bark was itself a valuable product and was hauled back to the mill with the timber. The logs were tied together one after the other with heavy ropes or cables. These were then dragged by oxen teams over "skid roads" twelve to fifteen feet wide and used to skid or drag logs through woods to the mill. A load might consist of as many as eight to ten log segments.

The operation focused on the bottom of the canyon. "When my great-grandfather logged it, he didn't go up very high on the canyon walls. There's no way they could get those trees all the way down easily, so they logged mostly the flat of the canyon," Marty McCormick explained. "They pretty much took everything out except for a few selected trees. Of course, the growth today is all back."

Unluckily, Hamilton was killed on December 6, 1885, when he was struck by a chunk of stone from the disintegration of the lumber mill's high-speed flywheel. Despite the tragedy, the mill continued to operate; it ceased operations sometime between 1905 and 1909. James passed away in 1919 at the age of eighty. "James McCormick is one of the most prominent figures in the public life of the county," an obituary remarked. "He has served as road supervisor, deputy assessor and later was a member of the San Mateo County Exposition Commission. He owns valuable timber lands and his mercantile business is now the leading store in his district."

Butano is filled with sagas of other logging operations. The focus of most early lumbering in the area appears to have been along Gazos Creek. The Birch and Steen shingle mill was located just west of the confluence of Bear Creek and Gazos Creek and about five miles from the ocean. This enterprise was sold to Horace Templeton, who moved the mill upstream and organized it as the Pacific Lumber and Mill Company.

Lumber was floated down a flume to the intersection of Cloverdale Road and Gazos Creek Road, where it was hauled to Pigeon Point for shipping. In February 1873, forty-nine-year-old Judge Templeton fell down a cliff, struck his head and was seriously injured. None of the doctors at his bedside could cure the "violent pain in his head," and he died ten days later. The mill closed following his death.

During the same period, a machinist named William M. Taylor built a shingle mill on the south bank of Little Butano Creek. Partnering with William Jackson, Taylor operated the mill for almost ten years. In 1882, James McKinley, brother of the future president, reactivated the Pacific Lumber mill. Eventually, the venture was renamed the McKinley Mill and was soon supplying the increasingly powerful and expanding Southern Pacific Railroad.

"Shingle King"

Also in the 1880s, Sheldon Purdy Pharis purchased property in the upper Little Butano basin. He also acquired the Taylor mill and owned or constructed several others. As did so many others, he moved from New York, in 1853 at age twenty-five, in search of gold. He had little success and found himself broke. With an axe, a saw and a mule, he began making shingles from readily available redwood scraps considered useless by the lumbermen.

Over time, Pharis was noted as an innovator in the logging industry, improving methods and adding new processes to his mills. Mill vendors

In the 1880s, Purdy Pharis was known far and wide as the "Shingle King." He was a noted innovator in the logging industry. *Daily Journal* (San Mateo, CA).

nationwide knew his work. He became known far and wide as the "Shingle King." It was estimated that from his beginnings in Santa Cruz in 1863 and into the 1880s, he manufactured and sold three hundred million shingles.

Despite his successes, on March 1, 1884, Pharis committed suicide. He was only fifty-five years old. Soon after, the mill ceased operation. "The death of S.P. Pharis casts a gloom over the entire county. Expressions of sadness are everywhere," one newspaper account revealed. "He was endowed with a kind heart and a generous nature. In cases of need, he always responded heartily."

Purdy lived simply, was a loner and a bachelor. He loved the outdoors and was perhaps a bit eccentric. Yet he was unselfish and well thought of by his associates. On the morning of his death, he was visited by a respected local dentist, Dr.

Tripp, who reported him in an "unbalanced condition." What that meant was never fully explained. What is known is that the doctor was summoned by a nearby resident, Hiram Haskins. Haskins had been a stage driver in Arizona. He was not particularly well liked and had a reputation as being "gruff, unruly, rough and tumble, used to using strong-arm tactics."

The night before, Purdy had two house guests: Emanuel Stevens, a relative stranger to the area, and Hiram Haskins. According to the testimony of Stevens and Haskins at the coroner's jury, "After Pharis retired to his room, they heard a sound that sounded like a boot on the floor. This was followed by some moaning. They called out to him to see if he was sick but he called back 'no'. In the morning, the two guests broke in his door and found him on the floor. His revolver lay in front of him."

Questions about Purdy's death continued to linger. "The bullet entered Purdy's head from the rear. While it was deemed physically possible, it does seem improbable for a man to shoot himself from behind," a local newspaper declared. "Since Haskins lived in a larger house nearby, why had he spent the night? The sound of a gun would be louder than a dropping shoe, wouldn't it? Why had a loner like Pharis chosen to commit suicide when guests were in the house?"

Many have wondered about a motive. A primary possibility has surfaced over the years. When Purdy's will was settled, he left his property to a variety of charities and distant relatives. One person purchased all of the property from the family members: Hiram Haskins. Some believe that he may have been conducting a campaign to convince people of Purdy's lunacy, then use that as a screen to mask murder and make a land grab.

BUTANO STATE PARK

Butano State Park was created in 1957 to protect redwoods on the California coast from logging. Today's visitors to the park will find quiet canyons filled with towering redwoods of the second and third growths. The park has a dozen hiking trails winding through canyons and plateaus and along chattering creeks. Scattered throughout are patches of oak forest, wet riparian and sunny chaparral ecosystems. Among the diverse wildlife and plants in the park are woodpeckers, water lizards, wildflowers and calypso orchids that bloom in the spring.

A unique resident is the endangered marbled murrelet. "The seabird is part of the auk family, which includes puffins, razorbills and auklets,

The Candelabra Tree is an old-growth redwood at Butano State Park. It has five huge stems extending from a large trunk. *California State Parks.*

murrelets dive underwater in the ocean to feed on anchovies and sardines," a park naturalist explained. "What makes these birds special, however, is that while all other auks nest on seaside cliffs and bluffs, the murrelet nests inland in old-growth redwoods and Douglas firs."

There are fern-lined trails that climb up past fragrant bay laurels and oaks before reaching a section of hardy, wind-sculpted Douglas firs. There are gorgeous trails running along Little Butano Creek. Thick forests sometimes lead to panoramic views of the valley or glimpses of the ocean. A special feature of the park is the Candelabra Trail, which hides an old-growth redwood that is truly spectacular. The tree is named for its five huge stems that extend from a trunk that is twenty feet in diameter.

Butano's unusual, single candelabra tree was probably spared from the axes because loggers were seeking straight redwood trunks for perfect wood planks. Those could not be gotten from the candelabra, with its distorted shape caused by its "reiterated trunk." This kind of tree begins as a single trunk that grows upward. However, at about ten to twelve feet, it splits into branches that begin horizontal to the ground then twist vertically to continue growing upward.

Resembling a Douglas fir, the candelabra once flourished in the northern hemisphere. Now it is commonly found along the coast from Big Sur to Oregon, in the cool, moist climate it needs to flourish. If left undisturbed, the tree can live to two thousand years or more. It is estimated that Butano's tree is more than two hundred years old. People describe the tree as magical, spiritual, inspiring and breathtaking.

There is something special about the bounty and beauty of the trees, the everlasting nature of redwoods found only on the West Coast. Redwoods are a symbol of regrowth and renewal. They are splendid examples of strength and forgiving. In many ways, they are ageless symbols of our past, protectors of our present and sentinels of our future.

7

PIGEON POINT LIGHT STATION STATE HISTORIC PARK

PHINEAS F. MARSTON, MASTER BUILDER

F amous for its towering lighthouse, Pigeon Point Light Station sits high atop the bluffs of Pescadero and became a State Historic Park in 1980. Pigeon Point was named for a shipwreck that occurred in 1853 during the gold rush era. Twenty years later, Phineas F. Marston was the master builder responsible for overseeing the completion of a lighthouse to guide ships to safety.

MARITIME WEST

Rock-strewn and foggy, Pigeon Point's waters are filled with treacherous hazards. Submerged rocks, swirling currents and back eddies present a challenge even for expert seamen. This part of the coast became known to mariners as exceptionally dangerous. In the persistent, thick haze, navigational readings were unreliable and signals from foghorns and other ships were easily misinterpreted.

When gold was discovered in California in 1848, fortune hunters and ships alike flooded into the state. Far more people came by sea than overland, and the Pacific coast was soon known as the "Maritime West." Ships of all kinds brought hundreds of ambitious settlers and merchants along with tons of sugar, coffee, whiskey, foodstuffs, tools and supplies. As ship traffic increased along California's shores, so did the number of shipwrecks.

After the clipper ship *Carrier Pigeon* wrecked at Whale Point in 1853, the area became known as Pigeon Point. *Mystic Seaport.*

The first recorded shipwreck at what was then called Whale Point was in 1853. On its maiden voyage from Boston to San Francisco, the clipper ship *Carrier Pigeon* was thrown off course and crashed into the rocks. Fortunately, all aboard survived. Scavengers swarmed the beach, stripping copper from the ship's hull and carrying off food, merchandise and other valuable cargo.

Two days after the wreck, a steamer arrived to begin salvaging efforts, but the captains bickered over how to proceed. The next day, another ship, the *Sea Bird*, arrived and was pitched onto the rocks next to the *Carrier Pigeon*. Two days after that, Captain Robert "Bully" Waterman arrived. Waterman had been charged with brutality on another ship, and controversy over his reputation hindered salvage efforts even more. Eventually, 1,200 packages of merchandise were saved.

The events surrounding the *Carrier Pigeon*'s wreck were so unforgettable that Whale Point was renamed Pigeon Point. During the 1860s, other ships and many lives were lost, prompting a public outcry for lighthouses to be built. In 1872, a lighthouse was finally erected at Pigeon Point. Noted engineer Phineas F. Marston was selected to guide the construction.

Growing Reputation

Phineas Frost Marston was born in Auburn, Maine, in 1813. Into his twenties, he remained close to his family, working a farm that supplied grain and produce. He also began studying the carpenter's trade. In 1833, Phineas moved to Bangor, Maine, where he was employed as a journeyman carpenter. According to one historian, "He was dedicated to becoming a skilled tradesman and eagerly applied himself to the work."

Bangor was an important lumber port surrounded by over three hundred sawmills. Although sailors and loggers gave the city a widespread reputation for roughness, Bangor proudly boasted the title "Lumber Capital of the World." Timber was harvested in the northern Maine woods and floated down the Penobscot River to Bangor. Often, the river was so swollen with logs that people could walk from one shore to the other.

By 1838, Phineas was building churches, army barracks and railroad depots throughout New England. As his reputation expanded, he gained influential clients. They included merchant Shepard Cary, for whom he constructed a flour mill in Maine. Cary was a powerful figure with extensive lumber operations, agricultural holdings and mercantile pursuits. In 1840, he began constructing a group of mills near Houlton that became known as Cary's Mills. Included was a gristmill, sawmill, clapboard mill, machine shop and furniture shop, all with the best available machinery.

Phineas also designed an elaborate home for Wentworth Winslow, the high sheriff at Woodstock in New Brunswick. Located close to the U.S.-Canada border and Houlton, Maine, the area was a prosperous seaport filled with lumber mills and shipbuilding facilities. Winslow described his resulting residence as "beautifully situated and possessing most of the conveniences which a country gentleman could desire."

Phineas was also called on to create the new railway buildings at Bangor for the Penobscot & Kennebec Railroad Company. On its completion in 1855, Bangor had its first connection by iron rail with Portland, Maine, a well-known commercial port and shipbuilding center.

The Presidio and Angel Island

In 1858, Phineas sailed to California with his wife, Susan Elizabeth Fisher, and four children. The initial part of the trip was made from New York to Panama aboard the noteworthy steamship *Star of the West*. Built in 1852 for business magnate Cornelius Vanderbilt, the vessel was later part of the United States Mail Steamship Company fleet. After the family crossed the Isthmus of Panama, the second leg of their voyage was on the popular steamship *Golden Gate*. Built by the distinguished William Webb in 1851, the vessel was part of the flourishing Pacific Mail Steamship Company.

Upon arriving in San Francisco, Phineas enlisted the help of his older brother Sylvanus to build a family home. Also in California was his old friend Colonel Edwin B. Babbitt, who was stationed with the Third Artillery at the San Francisco Presidio. Babbitt hired Phineas as superintendent of construction to build new barracks at the Presidio and an adjacent military installation at Camp Reynolds.

The Presidio was a military post located at the northern tip of the San Francisco peninsula. Established by the Spanish in 1776, the facility grew into a significant center for assembling and training American military forces. Camp Reynolds was a sheltered cove on the west side of Angel Island developed in 1863 to enhance Union coastal defenses during the Civil War.

Phineas was hired to construct the camp's first buildings, which consisted of one set of company quarters and another of officers' quarters. However, the project did not progress smoothly. First Lieutenant Louis H. Fine, who commanded the base, sent numerous complaints about Phineas to the adjutant general in San Francisco.

Lieutenant Fine complained that the quarters were "unfinished although Marston had been working for a month with ten men." There may have been other reasons for the strain between the two men. It's interesting to note that early in 1864, Fine was replaced by Major George Andrews. Then, over a thirteen-month period between 1867 and 1868, Fine was convicted twice with being "so much under the influence of liquor as to be unable to perform any military duty."

EDIZ HOOK AND POINT REYES

While he was working on projects at the Presidio, Phineas caught the attention of Lieutenant Colonel Robert S. Williamson. Williamson, a graduate of the U.S. Military Academy, was an accomplished engineer. Initially, he served with the U.S. Army Corps of Topographical Engineers, later known as the Corps of Engineers, and conducted surveys for proposed routes for the transcontinental railroad in California and Oregon.

In 1863, Williamson became the lighthouse engineer for the Twelfth District Lighthouse Board. Known for his meticulous nature, he worked on lighthouses, defenses and harbors along the Pacific coast. Impressed with Phineas's work, Williamson called on him to assume the position of superintendent of buildings for the Twelfth District.

Phineas's first project was at Ediz Hook. Located in Washington, the three-and-a-half-mile sandspit protects Port Angeles, the deepest harbor in the Northwest. The "Hook" was created by wind and tidal action along the southern edge of the strait. The sandspit creates a natural harbor to the south, sheltering the area off Port Angeles from the large ocean-sourced swells that roll eastward.

Completed in 1865, the lighthouse was a two-story, schoolhouse-type building with a lighthouse tower arising at one end of its gabled roof. Previously, only a "bonfire beacon" consisting of driftwood burned atop a tripod provided light for navigation. A second Ediz Hook lighthouse was constructed near the first one in 1908, with the two buildings existing in proximity to each other.

In 1870, Phineas returned to California to oversee the construction of a lighthouse and fog signal at Point Reyes. Located thirty miles northwest of San Francisco, a lighthouse was assigned to Point Reyes in 1855, but construction was delayed because of a dispute between the U.S. Lighthouse Board and the landowners over a fair price for the property.

Due to concerns that heavy fog could obscure the lighthouse, it was perched on a ledge 275 feet down a steep bluff. "Point Reyes is the windiest place on the Pacific Coast and the second-foggiest place on the North American continent," one report explained. "The Point Reyes Headlands, which jut ten miles out to sea, pose a threat to each ship entering or leaving San Francisco Bay."

PIGEON POINT

Phineas's work along the San Mateo coast began in 1871 with the construction of Pigeon Point Lighthouse. For the previous decade, the U.S. Lighthouse Board had been under constant attack by shippers, navigators and chambers of commerce across the country. All complained of the inadequate lighthouse system. Beleaguered by internal politics, the board was slow in overcoming its deficiencies and placing emphasis on new lighthouse locations.

Phineas Marston completed a lighthouse, fog signal building and keepers' home at Pigeon Point in 1872. Today, it is a treasured landmark. *U.S. Coast Guard.*

Finally, enough pressure was exerted on the U.S. Lighthouse Board to build a fog signal station and lighthouse at Pigeon Point. At the end of 1868, Congress appropriated $90,000 for the purpose. Two years later, the site was purchased, along with nearby Año Nuevo Island. By June 1871, Phineas and his crew were working on the lighthouse tower, keepers' dwelling and fog signal building.

Progress on the beacon was well publicized in the local press. The *San Mateo Times-Gazette* reported: "In company with Phineas F. Marston, lighthouse constructor, we visited the site of the projected lighthouse at Pigeon Point and found that operations have already commenced. The tower is to be built of brick and men are already at work making them."

In September 1871, the fog signal went into service and significant progress was being made on the keepers' house. The original dwelling was a Victorian duplex with a shed outbuilding. Around 1900, a rear addition was built, creating a fourplex. Divided into four separate apartments, the home was designed to accommodate a head keeper and three assistant keepers.

On November 15, 1872, Pigeon Point Lighthouse first displayed its brilliant rays. A local newspaper reported, "On Friday night, at sunset, lampist Thomas J. Winship lit the lamp at Pigeon Point Light Station and it became a vital navigation aid on California's central coast."

Of the twenty-six towers constructed in California after 1856, Pigeon Point was one of only four to be made of brick. A double-wall construction with an air space between insulates interior ironwork against corrosion. Over five hundred thousand locally made bricks were used to assure that the tower would be sturdy and durable.

The sentinel and Phineas Marston's efforts are still being appreciated. According to a recent historic structures report: "Pigeon Point has long been considered the most beautiful and best architectural lighthouse structure on the Pacific Coast. It is a superb example of the mid-nineteenth century traditional, classic lighthouse and an impressive landmark."

The 115-foot sentinel and its surrounding grounds have been preserved as the Pigeon Point Light Station State Historic Park. The lighthouse was listed in the National Register of Historic Places in 1977 and was designated in 1980 as a California Historical Landmark.

AÑO NUEVO AND POINT MONTARA

At the same time Phineas was overseeing efforts at Pigeon Point, he was supervising activities at nearby Año Nuevo. After the wreck of the clipper ship *Carrier Pigeon* in 1853, the U.S. Lighthouse Board surveyed the area for possible lighthouse locations. Surveyors considered a station on Año Nuevo Island, which was connected to the mainland by a sandbar at low tide. However, Año Nuevo Point was more accessible, at a higher elevation and more stable.

In 1857, plans were developed for a lighthouse at Año Nuevo Point but were never executed. Difficulties acquiring land and the outbreak of the Civil War delayed further progress until the 1870s. At the same time Pigeon Point's tower was being completed, a fog signal station with a steam whistle was placed at Año Nuevo Point. A keepers' dwelling was constructed at the southern end of Año Nuevo Island, with a wooden walkway running north to the fog signal station.

In 1875, Phineas completed a fog signal station and keepers' quarters at Point Montara. Located about twenty-five miles north of Pigeon Point, Point Montara sits only seventy feet above the sea. Along this foggy, final approach to San Francisco, many ships were forced to hug the perilous coast, putting them in danger of rocky outcroppings and unruly seas.

Phineas Marston finished a fog signal station and keepers' dwelling at Año Nuevo in 1872. Now, marine life occupies the keepers' residence. *Julie Barrow.*

Shortly after Point Montara's completion, Phineas retired to his ranch in Alameda, where he cultivated fruits, vegetables and flowers. He passed away in 1896 at the age of eighty-three, leaving an indelible mark in history and on lighthouses along the Pacific coast. "He was an exceptionally skilled carpenter," his great-great-granddaughter Barbara Houghton noted. "He was also known as a man of unflinching honesty and was highly respected for all that he did."

COMMEMORATING MARITIME HISTORY

Even a lighthouse could not prevent shipwrecks. Over the years, human error and unpredictable weather led to other maritime tragedies. One of those events, commemorated at Pigeon Point, is a constant reminder of the dangers of the sea.

Steadfast schooners like the *Point Arena* were the mainstay of local maritime economy. For over two decades, the tireless little ship wandered California's coast, hauling tons of lumber and freight to and from "dog hole" ports like

The *Point Arena* wrecked at Pigeon Point in 1913. The schooner's broken bow is a reminder of the dangers of the sea. *JoAnn Semones.*

Pigeon Point. Seasoned seafarers claimed that the nickname grew out of the fact that there was "hardly enough room enough for a dog to turn around in one of those." Others insisted it came from the fact that each cove had a resident dog. Making their way up the coast in heavy fog, schooner captains navigated by memorizing each distinctive bark.

Although the stories are surely exaggerated, there is no doubt that operating in these precarious coves was risky at best. It took great skill to maneuver in tight spaces in proximity to rocky shores. A sudden gust of wind or errant swell could catch even the most stalwart ship by surprise.

In the early morning hours of August 9, 1913, despite strong southeast winds and choppy seas, *Point Arena* began loading its cargo manifested for San Francisco. Unexpectedly, the schooner fouled a mooring line in its propeller. Although the captain tried for deeper water, the wind caught its stern. The defenseless ship lurched violently, slamming broadside into the rocks and tearing its deck in half. Luckily, the crew survived. What remained of the ship was burned as a navigation hazard. A local resident mused, "It would not have looked good to have a wrecked ship in front of a lighthouse."

In 1983, a five-ton fragment of the hull washed ashore and is on display at Pigeon Point. Other artifacts and exhibits at Pigeon Point can be seen in the interpretive center and in the old fuel bunker. You can immerse yourself in stories about Pigeon Point's early inhabitants, Portuguese shore whaling station and shipping center. You can also enjoy shipwreck tales, keepers' stories and learn the impact of World War II. It's topped off with the ability to view the iconic first-order Fresnel lens on display in the fog signal building. The experience is no less than being able to sail back through 150 years of amazing maritime history.

8

AÑO NUEVO STATE PARK

THE STEELE FAMILY, DETERMINED DAIRY FARMERS

A lthough well known for its large elephant seal population, Año Nuevo State Park's history includes many human aspects. The Steeles were one of the earliest and most significant families to settle in Pescadero. Vestiges of the Steele Brothers Dairy, including old barns and other historic buildings, are still visible on park property. During World War II, Año Nuevo was part of an early-warning system to protect U.S. shores.

SOLDIER AND BROTHER

Frederick B. Steele was the first member of his family drawn to California. Born in New York in 1819, he graduated from West Point in 1843. One of his classmates was Ulysses S Grant, the future Civil War hero. After distinguishing himself for bravery during the Mexican-American War, Frederick was promoted to first lieutenant in 1848.

Between 1850 and 1853, Frederick fought in California during the Yuma War. The conflict consisted of a series of U.S. military operations conducted in Southern California and what is now southwestern Arizona. During a visit to Ohio, he urged his family to relocate to California. According to one source, "He told his brothers, in glowing terms, of the beauties and promises of the golden land."

Frederick received his captain's commission in 1855, and when the Civil War broke out in 1861, he was appointed a major in the U.S. Infantry. In

1863, he participated in the Siege of Vicksburg. The city was the last major Confederate stronghold on the Mississippi River. With no reinforcement and supplies nearly gone and after holding out for more than forty days, the rebel garrison finally surrendered on July 4. A monument to Frederick stands on the grounds of Vicksburg National Military Park.

As the war continued, Frederick rose to the rank of general. In June 1865, he was transferred to Texas to command forces along the Rio Grande. In November 1867, he took a leave of absence from his military duties. Two months later, Frederick Steele passed away from a stroke he suffered during a buckboard race. He was only forty-eight years old.

Pioneer Dairymen

Following discussions with their brother Frederick, Isaac C., George H. and Edgar W. Steele left their home in Ohio for California. George and his cousin Rensselaer arrived in 1855, first working in mines in San Francisco. Within a year, they found a farm to rent north of San Francisco at Two Rocks in Petaluma.

They were joined by George's parents, brother Edgar and Rensselaer's family in 1856. From wages earned harvesting oats, Edgar purchased five cows. The family began making butter and planted eighty acres of grain and potatoes. In 1857, Isaac took his family to Two Rocks.

Despite an industry downturn, Rensselaer's wife, Clarissa, made a cheese from a recipe in her grandmother's old cookbook and sent the product to a commission house in San Francisco. Her recipe was so well received that it found a huge demand in the city. The Steeles expanded their small dairy business by adding twenty-five cows and then began looking for suitable grazing land at the moist coastal headlands of Point Reyes. Their dairy would become one of the first commercial dairies in the United States.

During the initial year of operation, the Steeles made more than fifty-five thousand pounds of cheese at a value of nearly $15,000. In 1859, they reported that they had made $6,000 in improvements on the ranch, milked 163 cows during the season and hired nine men to work the dairy. The operation had expanded into three dairies consisting of 355 cows. "Butter was sold readily at a dollar per pound and cheese at twenty-seven cents," Edgar said. "Demand was greater than we could supply."

By 1861, over six hundred cows were grazing on the Steeles' land, and the family could boast a cash profit of $10,000. Their operations were the most

In 1864, the Steele family created a huge block of cheese, gaining national attention. They sent a piece to President Abraham Lincoln. *Library of Congress.*

prominent and extensive in the county, producing more cheese than any dairy in the state. With the herds increasing, larger quantities of cheese were shipped by steamer to San Francisco about every ten days. Cash accounts revealed the nature of products that were brought back to the Steele ranch from San Francisco. They included brandy, smoked salmon, vegetables, clothing, sarsaparilla and even a Steinway piano.

SAWMILLS AND SHIPPING

Dissatisfied that the Point Reyes land they leased was not for sale, the Steeles surveyed the coast south of San Francisco for additional pasturage. In 1862, they leased land from Loren Coburn at Rancho Punto del Año Nuevo and immediately began construction on five dairies. They included Pocket Dairy at Pebble Beach Hill; Whitehouse Canyon; Green Oaks, run by Isaac; Cascade, run by Rensselaer; and Cloverdale, run by Edgar. While the main product was cheese, butter was produced in the dry season.

Soon after arriving, the Steeles gave William W. Waddell a right-of-way across their land in order to build a landing and wharf. Waddell, who lived nearby, had built a sawmill on his property in hopes of finding an efficient way to transport the lumber to market. He constructed the wharf about five hundred yards west of Año Nuevo Creek, where the water was deep but safe.

Waddell completed the seven-hundred-foot wharf in 1864, including a swinging chute at the end to serve waiting schooners. Three years later, the wharf was handling two million feet of lumber per year. By the 1870s, the Steeles had constructed a sawmill on Año Nuevo Creek, hauling lumber to Waddell's wharf. Rensselaer built another mill in the canyon above his home at Cascade Ranch.

"The wharf is high above the force of the surf at highest tide," the *Daily Alta* reported. "By means of a slide, vessels are loaded rapidly and dispatched quickly to San Francisco. Schooners also load here for San Pedro and San Luis Obispo."

For the next thirteen years, the wharf served Waddell's mill, the Steeles' dairies and mills and others in the region. A lumberyard, warehouse, general store, post office and several additional buildings were constructed at the landing near the wharf. The little settlement soon became known as Waddell's Landing.

PRIME PASTURELAND

In the mid-1860s, the Steeles also purchased property in Southern California at San Luis Obispo. They paid about $1.10 an acre for the Corral de Piedra (Stone Corral), Pismo, Bolsa de Chamizal (Chamisal) and Arroyo Grande Ranchos. Edgar and George moved to the area, where they introduced dairy farming on forty-five thousand acres of prime pastureland.

One year, Edgar undertook an experiment with 150 milking stock. He knew that the statewide production average was twenty-five pounds of milk for every pound of butter and ten pounds of milk for each pound of cheese. His goal was to surpass that average, and the results were amazing. Working day and night over a three-day period, he produced a pound of butter with every seventeen pounds of milk and a pound of cheese with every eight pounds of milk. While he couldn't sustain such an intense effort, he hoped to increase both his herd and his number of farmhands.

Unfortunately, after years of legal troubles, much of the land was sold, but George and Edgar continued to be active in the community. Edgar was one of the incorporators of the San Luis Obispo Water Company and president of the Bank of San Luis Obispo. He also held a seat on the Granger's Business Association. Edgar remained in San Luis Obispo until his death at age sixty-six in 1896.

George was a practicing lawyer. He was elected to the convention that framed the California Constitution and served on the Judiciary Committee and the Committee on Corporations. He was elected as the Republican candidate for state senator from the San Luis District, serving from 1884 to 1888. He died in San Luis Obispo at age eighty-seven in 1912.

MAMMOTH CHEESE

At Año Nuevo, devotion to Frederick prompted the Steeles to make a unique contribution to the 1864 Mechanic's Fair in San Francisco. They created a "monstrous" block of cheese, which gained national attention. "This mammoth cheese was the product of the dairies over two days," one report explained. "A gigantic hoop and press were made for the purpose, and novel appliances were required to handle the great weight and safely transport it to San Francisco."

The cheese, which was eighteen inches thick, twenty feet in circumference and weighed 3,850 pounds, was cited for its "perfect form and beauty." Pieces of it were cut and sent to President Abraham Lincoln and General Ulysses S Grant. The rest of the block sold for $1 a pound, realizing nearly $3,000 in proceeds, which were donated to the U.S. Sanitary Commission of the Union army. The forerunner of the Red Cross, the agency was created in 1861 to support sick and wounded soldiers of the Civil War.

In 1866, the original lease at Año Nuevo expired. Loren Coburn retained control of the Pocket and Cloverdale dairies, while Isaac remained at Green

Catherine Steele sits at one of two picnic tables made from the crate holding a 3,850-pound cheese. *Santa Cruz Museum of Art & History.*

Oaks and Rensselaer at Cascade. The Steeles expanded their holdings by purchasing an additional seven thousand acres running south to the Santa Cruz County line.

By 1867, their landholdings contained eleven ranches. They managed one thousand dairy cows, which supplied San Francisco with thousands of pounds of dairy products each week. When the south coast became part of San Mateo County in 1868, the Steeles easily became the most important dairymen in the county.

According to one historian, "The success that attended the Steele family furnishes a notable example of what may be accomplished in California through industry and intelligent application of labor, even when they begin with small means."

The Steeles continued to prosper, selling both cheese and butter. By the early 1870s, the Steele Brothers were reportedly the second-largest owners of milk cows in the state. In 1876, Isaac became a founding member of the California State Dairymen's Association. One newspaper pointed out, "The organization is valuable for uniting dairymen and for improving dairy methods and practices."

AURA OF TIMELESSNESS

Rensselaer Jr. was forced to sell his land in 1919 to his attorney, who put roughly half of the acreage under cultivation growing artichokes, tomatoes, rice, corn and tobacco. Although the ranch went through several transitions, it continued to produce a variety of crops until 1943.

At that time, a fire engulfed much of Cascade Ranch, destroying a large barn and several smaller buildings. Luckily, the original 1862 dairy building survived. Soon after the blaze, new buildings were constructed, and they still stand today. In 1986, the Trust for Public Land purchased 4,088 acres and then sold 2,914 acres to California State Parks. The acquisition contained about half of the original Cascade Ranch headquarters. Today, it is part of Año Nuevo State Park.

Isaac maintained large-scale dairy operations at Green Oaks until his death in 1903. At this time, the holdings were divided among his three children. His daughter Effie married Edwin Dickerman, who worked at Waddell's wharf. Their part of Green Oaks became known as the Dickerman Ranch. It survives today as the Año Nuevo State Park headquarters.

Although the Steeles produced cheese into the 1940s, they shifted to farming field crops in the 1930s. William Steele, Isaac's grandson, continued to be active on the ranch until his death in 1953. In 1967, William's widow, Catherine Baumgarten Steele, made a gift of the Green Oaks Ranch to the county of San Mateo to be used for historical and educational purposes. However, the county later sold the ranch to private parties. In 2006, the Peninsula Open Space Trust purchased the ranch. Fortunately, the ranch is now part of Año Nuevo State Park.

"The Steeles were the first permanent American settlers at Año Nuevo," Catherine Steele commented. "They established homes that are still standing today, lending the aura of timelessness that lingers over the scenically beautiful and historic area."

EARLY-WARNING SYSTEM

During World War II, lighthouse beacons across America were extinguished to protect the country's borders from possible attack. Since lighthouses were placed strategically along the nation's shoreline, the U.S. Coast Guard established lookout stations at many of the sites. One of them was at the Año Nuevo Island lighthouse. Seaman First Class Arthur H. Smith Jr., a member of the lookout crew, declared, "Everyone was scared stiff."

Art, who had longed to join the Coast Guard since age fourteen, enlisted on December 8, 1941, the day after Pearl Harbor was bombed. On his arrival at Año Nuevo in April 1942, he was introduced to Bernice Steele Taylor, a granddaughter of dairy rancher Isaac Steele. In the 1860s, Isaac Steele and his brothers operated a series of Bay Area dairies, including one

Año Nuevo Island was a Coast Guard lookout station during World War II to help protect America's shores from possible attack. *U.S. Coast Guard.*

at Año Nuevo. Until the 1940s, their enterprise was a dominant producer of cheese and butter, mostly for export to San Francisco.

"It was just a week before my nineteenth birthday and she knew I was feeling a little homesick," Art confessed, "so she baked me a cake."

The Coast Guard lookout shack was at the very tip of Año Nuevo Island. The post was manned twenty-four hours a day, seven days a week. While one crew member was on liberty, the others worked in shifts of four hours on, eight hours off.

The lookout crew had three primary duties: to detect and observe enemy vessels and airplanes operating in coastal waters; to transmit information on these craft to command headquarters; and to report attempts of landings by the enemy. "Using binoculars, we scanned the horizon for any lights, ships, or planes," Art explained. "It all had to be reported by crank telephone to headquarters in San Francisco."

Once, a submarine was detected just south of Año Nuevo by a group of local fishermen. They thought they spotted a submarine periscope and reported it. Supposedly, the area was bombed. Rumors persisted for years that a German or Japanese sub lay in the water close to shore.

There was ample cause for concern. Shortly after the attack on Pearl Harbor, Japanese submarines were dispatched to shell selected U.S. coastal towns and lighthouses. Several ships were torpedoed within sight of California cities, including the eight-thousand-ton tanker *Montebello* off the coast of Cambria, about 185 miles south of Año Nuevo. The crew was unarmed, yet as the men jumped into lifeboats, a submarine surfaced, firing with its deck gun. The *Montebello* stood on its bow and slid beneath the sea.

Most of Año Nuevo's supplies were delivered by the buoy tender USS *Lupine*. Built as a mine planter for the army in 1918, the *Lupine* was converted to a U.S. Lighthouse Service tender and commissioned on April 14, 1927. Art noted, "She operated out of San Francisco all along the California coast."

Sometimes, Art brought groceries, mail and supplies from nearby Pescadero to the island. Mrs. Taylor graciously offered the use of her horse and buggy. "I'd harness up old Dolly, drive her down to the beach and unload the boxes into a dory to row out to the island," Art recalled. "Then, I patted her on the bottom and she trotted back to the barn on her own."

When the Coast Guard needed additional men for active duty in August 1942, Art volunteered. He served as a gunner's mate aboard *LST-202*. The vessel carried twelve tanks and six hundred troops. Known as "giant sea-going freight cars," LSTs were designed to support amphibious operations by carrying huge loads of military vehicles, cargo and troops. Art remarked, "We made all the Pacific invasions that General MacArthur did."

When the war ended, Art represented the Coast Guard by carrying the American flag in a parade in San Francisco. He beamed, "It was my second claim to fame."

The view from Año Nuevo Point to Año Nuevo Island is extraordinary. Although vestiges of the keepers' quarters and fog signal station building remain, no evidence of the lookout station exists. But on just the right day, in just the right light, you might catch sight of the ghosts of heroic young sailors safeguarding our shores.

9

RANCHO DEL OSO STATE PARK

THEODORE J. HOOVER, CONSERVATIONIST AND NATURALIST

Rancho del Oso is Spanish for "ranch of the bear." The Davenport site was pioneered by William Waddell, a well-known businessman, before it was acquired by Theodore J. Hoover in 1912. The property was kept by the Hoover family until it became a California State Park in 1977.

WILLIAM'S LANDING

William White Waddell always had a sense of adventure. Born in Mason County, Kentucky, to John T. and Eleanor Waddell, he began what would be an industrious life in 1818. In the mid-1830s, he married Elizabeth Bailey Hudson and moved to Lexington, Missouri, to explore business opportunities and to spend time with his cousin William Bradford Waddell.

Bradford invested in many schemes over the years. While his cousin was pursuing his own business interests, William amassed a large fortune through an assortment of mercantile ventures. Unluckily, a few investments went sour. "He soon found himself with a dry bank account and a thirst for a fresh start," a biographer revealed. "The golden hills of California beckoned."

Even before the gold rush, California was seen as a land of vast opportunity. William's greatest interest was in lumbering. In the late 1840s, he met Dennis Martin, an Irish immigrant. Dennis acquired property on which he built two of the earliest sawmills in San Mateo County. He soon added a warehouse as well as a schooner, which sailed out of what is now Redwood Landing. For three years, William managed Dennis's sawmill operations before moving on to work at William's Landing, west of Santa Cruz, in 1851.

Located at the mouth of Liddell Creek, William's Landing was one of the most important of the early north coast landings. The four Williams brothers—James, Squire, John and Isaac—purchased the adjacent Rancho Arroyo de la Laguna in 1847. They grew potatoes, built a sawmill and founded a landing to ship goods to Monterey.

"We bought a ranch, four and a half miles square, lying immediately on the Pacific Ocean. There is immense quantity of all kinds of timber—redwood, pine and live oak. There is little use to tell about the height of the trees, for they grow so high that we can hardly see the tops," John Williams wrote. "If we have no bad luck, we will have a saw mill up and sawing about three miles from the sea shore."

The landing contained a large cable, known as a hawser, hanging over the water. Its ends were attached to the cliffs that formed a small cove. Schooners would hitch themselves to the hawser so that loads of lumber, lime and agricultural produce could be lowered to the deck. An early newspaper stated, "Shipping is safe and easy."

Despite the best precautions, there were occasions when lives were lost while attempting to load a wildly pitching vessel. On July 12, 1857, two crewmen from a schooner drowned when they were knocked out of a small boat by the swaying hawser. On January 8, 1869, a small lumber and lime schooner was dashed on the rocks. The entire crew of five was lost. Sometime after the mishap, William's Landing was abandoned.

WADDELL'S LANDING

From 1851 to 1861, William operated a number of prominent mills before embarking on a project along the creek that still carries his name. He purchased Rancho del Oso, where he established his home. Then he built a mill known as "Big Gulch" and began developing his own shipping port for lumber.

According to one account, "The canyon provided a near perfect site for a sawmill with its dense stand of big redwoods and a gentle slope to the sea, several miles away, where schooners could be loaded with lumber."

Construction of the $30,000 project required the use of a million feet of lumber, which the mill had to produce. William placed his mill two and a half miles upstream from the coast. A wharf was built at the mouth of the creek with a railroad leading to it. However, exposed to the power of the Pacific

Ocean with its high winds and pounding surf, the wharf was soon crushed into kindling. An attempt to drive piles for a new pier revealed the presence of bedrock just beyond the sandy beach, so a new plan was developed.

The railroad was extended another two and a half miles up the coast to a cove near the more protected waters of Año Nuevo. The bluff was low, and the sea was free of menacing reefs. A seven-hundred-foot pier was completed in 1864, reaching from the bluff to deep water. A swinging chute at the end could be lowered to the deck of a waiting schooner. One newspaper stated, "It was efficiently designed, and by virtue of being elevated, the sea washed beneath it."

Blessed with a stand of timber "more extensive and compact" than any other on the north coast, William's mill was equipped to turn out either rough or finished lumber of all kinds. The lumber was loaded onto small flatcars and drawn by teams of four horses or mules, hitched single file. The animals hauled the lumber from William's mill over five miles of wooden rails.

Extensive stacks of lumber littered the wharf, which also contained a warehouse and a residence. By 1867, Waddell's wharf was handling two million feet of lumber a year. It served both his mill and surrounding mills for approximately thirteen years.

GRISLY ENCOUNTER

William continued his life and lumbering operations until 1875, when an extraordinary mishap interrupted his activities. In the 1870s, California's coastal mountain ranges were still home to many grizzly bears, as was Rancho del Oso. Admired for their size and strength, the fearsome carnivores could weigh over two thousand pounds. Their huge paws contained claws measuring two to four inches in length.

William Waddell operated an early Coastside lumber mill at Rancho del Oso. In 1875, he died after an attack by a grizzly bear. *McCrary family.*

"The grizzly bear was the most formidable terrestrial mammal in the coastal region. These fierce carnivores dominated the lowlands. The grizzly had great physical strength, sharp canines and long curved claws," one source explained. "The bear could outrun any man and even climb a tree after him. Most humans came out second best in any confrontation."

Frontiersmen like this one were often surprised by grizzly bears. The animals weighed over two thousand pounds and had claws four inches long. *Hugh Glass.*

They roamed freely, thriving in great valleys and low mountains. Often, they descended on ranches, hoping to make a tasty meal of the local livestock. Perturbed by the loss of valuable ranch animals, some men tried capturing the bears. Horsemen would ride to a place where grizzlies congregated, choose the largest, charge it from front and rear and attempt to lasso the bear from all directions.

"The usual response of the grizzly was to rise on its hind legs and strike at the ropes. If he could seize one, he would pull it toward himself, paw over paw, despite strenuous resistance by the horse," one writer declared. "Since the opposite end of the rope was attached to the saddle, the safety of the rider depended on the speed with which a companion could lasso one of the paws and gallop off to throw the bear down."

On October 1, 1875, William's only intention was hunting for deer. He and his friend John Bradley crossed over a ridge from Waddell Creek on land above his homestead. The pair separated, with William moving up the creek and John moving down. William had also taken his dog, which had run off over a hillside. Barking excitedly, the dog reappeared, pursued by a powerful grizzly bear. Roaring down the ravine, the grizzly seized William by the leg. His dog attacked from the rear, causing the bear to turn and leave, but William was badly mauled.

He fired his gun to bring John. Unable to walk, William was forced to wait for a horse to carry him home. Miraculously, he survived to tell the story to his closest friends and family. A doctor was summoned from Santa Cruz to tend his wounds and to amputate one of his arms. Sadly, William Waddell died a heartbreaking five days later at age fifty-seven from what can only be called a grisly encounter.

William's mill closed a few years after he passed away. The canyon remained quiet for some time except for the activities of an occasional tanbark cutter or shake maker. From the 1930s to the 1950s, sporadic lumber operations appeared, most notably that of the Big Creek Lumber Company.

"William Waddell was a man of large views, great enterprise, considerable wealth and unerring integrity," one biographer asserted. "It was said of him that in all his dealings, he never made a written contract. Those who knew him never demanded it, for his word was all that was necessary."

THE LURE OF WANDER-LUST

Theodore J. Hoover, called "Tad" as a child, was born in 1871 in the agricultural town of West Branch, Iowa. Shortly after his birth, his parents, Jesse and Hulda, moved into the two-room cottage where his younger siblings, Herbert and Maria, were born. Herbert would go on to serve as president of the United States from 1929 to 1933.

Jesse built a blacksmith shop, making him one of only three in a town of five hundred. Luckily, many residents owned horses, buggies and wagons that required repair. In 1879, Jesse sold the shop and started a new farm implement business. It was the first in town to manufacture barbed wire. Sadly, Jesse died of heart failure at the end of 1880. He was only thirty-four years old.

Theodore J. Hoover bought a majority of the Waddell Valley in 1912. He kept the name of his holdings as Rancho del Oso. *Britannica*.

Hulda supported the children by sewing and renting to boarders. She saved Jesse's insurance policy for the children's schooling. She also became a Quaker minister, traveling several times a year and preaching to Friends' Societies throughout the state. Each time she left town, the children stayed with relatives. On one trip, Hulda fell ill and never recovered. She died from typhoid fever in 1884 at the age of thirty-five.

After their parents' deaths, Theodore and Maria lived with their uncle Davis and aunt Maria Hoover in Hardin County, Iowa. Herbert was sent to another uncle, John Minthorn, in Newberg, Oregon. Although his uncle Davis offered Theodore a home and a chance to learn all about farming, Theodore did not see that as a brilliant future. He left to join his brother in Oregon in 1887. He wrote, "The west was still the land of romance in those days and the 'wander-lust' had a good grip."

When he completed his early education, Theodore moved on to Stanford University in California. There, he received a degree in geology and mining in 1901. From 1903 to 1919, he was manager or consulting engineer in the gold mines of California, western Australia, Mexico and Alaska. He was also an engineer or administrator of lead and silver mines in Burma and of copper mines in Finland and Russia. His business offices were in London and San Francisco.

Later, he served at Stanford University as a professor of mining and metallurgy and then as dean of the school of engineering. Along the way, he gained a reputation as a noted writer, conservationist and naturalist.

An Exceptional Home

Theodore married Mildred Crew Brooks in 1899 in San Francisco. Together they raised three daughters, Mildred, Hulda and Louise. After all of his travels, Theodore was seeking an exceptional place to call home. It had to be a location that matched his fervor for and dedication to nature and conservation.

Theodore bought a majority of the Waddell Valley in 1912 from more than a dozen small landowners. He built the "Brown House" in 1913 as a family vacation house and kept the name of his holdings as Rancho del Oso. The Brown House was built from heart redwood and based on features the family desired.

According to a description provided by Hulda: "Downstairs, there were two bedrooms and a bathroom, a large living-dining room, kitchen, pantry and root cellar. It was surrounded by a wide porch from which an outside stairway led to the upper porch and a huge unfinished room and bath.

This was the children's dormitory until it was later divided into four rooms along a hall."

In 1925, Theodore built a large Spanish-style residence referred to as the "Casa." It was positioned across the creek from the Brown House. The Casa had many of the intriguing characteristics of early Spanish dwellings, including dramatic arches, warm woods and a clay tile roof. The house provided coolness in summer and warmth in winter.

In 1928, a reporter visiting the family described the scene at the ranch. "The canyon in which the home is built is a perfect panorama of scenic beauty, a grand kaleidoscope of endless foliage, shrubs and trees with the Waddell Creek running through the estate," he effused. "The grand canyon is worth going many miles to see, and you agree with the poet: in such surroundings as this, my wearied soul would rest, in peaceful calm and tranquility."

"Sang Itself into My Heart"

Theodore Hoover died in 1955 at the age of eighty-four. Although the Casa was destroyed by fire in 1959, several of Theodore's heirs maintained residences at Rancho del Oso. California State Parks acquired approximately two-thirds of the original Rancho del Oso land, including Waddell Beach, from Hoover's daughters in 1977. This enabled the completion of the Skyline-to-the-Sea Trail, a loop that provides a sampling of the natural beauty that Rancho del Oso has to offer.

"Taking the Skyline to the Sea Bypass Trail and returning on Skyline to the Sea, hikers pass through riparian and coastal scrub habitat, Monterey Pine, mixed evergreen and coast redwood forest, with views of the Waddell Valley reaching out to the beach community and marsh habitat," a brochure explains. "Hikers will see one of the few old growth redwoods in the valley and depending on the season, newt crossings, wildflower displays, or yellow leaves carpeting the forest floor. From October to late April, this trail requires a crossing at Waddell Creek due to seasonal bridge removal."

In 1985, Hulda Hoover McLean resolved to create a way to share the wonders of the natural world she had enjoyed. She sold her personal residence and its forty-acre lot to the Sempervirens Fund. Established in 1900 as Sempervirens Club, the organization is California's oldest land trust. Its mission is to protect and permanently preserve coast redwoods (*Sequoia*

Hulda McLean Writes Hoover History

GENEALOGY OF THE HERBERT HOOVER FAMILY. By Hulda Hoover McLean. Stanford University's Hoover Institution. $10 hardbound, $8 paperback.

Nuggets of history gleam from the pages of Hulda Hoover McLean's book which comprises a search of 13 generations of the Hoover family.

The book was released this month as Volume 30 of bibliographical series by Stanford's Hoover Institution on War, Revolution and Peace.

Mrs. McLean is a niece of the late Herbert Hoover, 31st President of the U.S., and the daughter of Herbert's brother, the late Theodore Hoover. Theodore Jesse

field, served as U.S. administrator of war relief programs during both world wars, secretary of commerce, chief executive, and chairman of the two commissions bearing his name.

Among the Hoover ancestors were two governors of Massachusetts Bay Colony and Swiss emigrants who supplied money, grain and soldiers for the American Revolution.

Appearing 11 generations back in Mrs. McLean's genealogy is the name of Thomas Dudley who became governor of Massachusetts Bay Colony and a founder of Harvard College. Dudley's daughter, Ann, is generally accorded a place of her own in history

Hulda Hoover McLean is shown in this 1967 newspaper clip. She stayed involved with Rancho del Oso well into her nineties. *Santa Cruz Sentinel.*

sempervirens) forests, wildlife habitat, watersheds and other important natural features of California's Santa Cruz Mountains. The fund does this by purchasing land for protection and transferring it to state or local agencies.

When her home was passed on to California State Parks, Hulda became active in organizing the Waddell Creek Association. In cooperation with California State Parks, the group operates the Rancho del Oso Nature and History Center, helping to support its volunteer and educational programs.

"With a gorgeous courtyard garden and warming stone fireplace, the center might be the most charming visitor center in the state. The former home is staged with engaging, interactive displays that detail the park's wildlife and wildly diverse landscape," park publicity claims. "You'll also discover the many critters that call the valley home, from stealthy bobcats to the steelhead salmon that fill Waddell Creek to the bygone grizzly bears that informed the park's Spanish name."

Hulda served on the association's board of directors well into her nineties. She died in 2006 at the age of one hundred. In a memoir titled *Rancho del Oso—How It Was*, she recalled her early days on the ranch. Hulda wrote: "The first day was pure magic. I stood still in the field in front of the new house and absorbed into the spell of the valley—fragrance of earth and flowers, color, and motion of butterflies, clouds, rippling grass and dancing trees. Its music—song of birds, distant surf, wind in the forest— sang itself into my heart."

Today, we are fortunate to be able to share the same experience and, perhaps on an exceptional day, to hear the echo of the same melody.

10

WILDER RANCH STATE PARK

DELOSS D. WILDER, INVENTIVE DAIRY RANCHER

Located five miles north of the city of Santa Cruz, Wilder Ranch State Park was established in 1974. Although Deloss D. Wilder and his family were the longest-residing inhabitants, the ranch had an unusual array of other owners, including José Antonio Bolcoff, Moses Meder and Levi Balwin. Artifacts of each of their residencies on the property are evident today.

Rancho del Refugio

From 1791 to 1835, all of the land west of Mission Santa Cruz was called Rancho Arroyo del Matadero ("ranch of the streambed slaughtering ground"). The land supported operations of Mission Santa Cruz and was used for crop cultivation and raising cattle. Spanish missionaries fostered a breed of long-horned cattle that were sacrificed for their hides and tallow. These products were traded for supplies with ships entering coastal ports.

In the 1830s, the land was inherited by the three daughters of José Joaquin Castro, a member of the De Anza Expedition and prominent local settler. The property became known as Rancho del Refugio, denoting a "place of refuge or shelter." The oldest sister, Maria Candida Castro, and her husband, José Antonio Bolcoff, became the rancho's first titled owners of record in 1841.

The 1840s Bolcoff adobe is the oldest structure at Wilder Ranch State Park. It was built on the former Rancho del Refugio. *Hamilton Historical Records.*

Bolcoff was born Osip Volkov in Siberia, Russia, about 1795. At age nineteen, he sailed to California aboard a Russian fur-trading ship, disembarking at Monterey. In short order, he won himself a place in the town's Spanish society, working as an interpreter for the governor. In 1817, he converted to Roman Catholicism and was baptized with a Spanish name, José Antonio Bolcoff, at nearby Mission Soledad. In 1822, he married Maria Candida Castro at the Monterey Presidio Chapel.

They settled at Villa de Branciforte, one of the last of the secular pueblos founded by the Spanish. For a number of years, he was alcalde (mayor) there. Established in 1797, the pueblo stood on the eastern bluff of the San Lorenzo River, facing Mission Santa Cruz on the west. The settlement existed as a separate township until 1905, when it was annexed to the city of Santa Cruz.

On the rancho, Bolcoff built an adobe, which is the oldest standing structure at Wilder Ranch State Park. It was created around 1839, using roof tiles transported from old Santa Cruz Mission buildings. The ranch was widely known for its cabbage, potatoes, cheese, butter and buttermilk, which were traded as far north as San Francisco.

"Bolcoff dairy ranch may have been the first of its kind in the region. Dairying was an unusual practice in California during the Spanish and

Mexican periods," one source explains. "Generally, the typical range cattle rounded up for their hides and tallow were poor milk producers, in addition to being very difficult to milk."

He had other business ventures. In particular, he began a partnership in 1848 to build a sawmill. Bolcoff supplied the land and the timber and half the construction costs in trade for one-half ownership. The sawmill was completed in 1849 and prospered because of the gold rush and the accompanying need for timber. Five years later, Bolcoff converted it into a flour mill.

Throughout his lifetime, Bolcoff was a smuggler, mostly peddling illegal goods from Russian ships. Over the years, he was arrested more than once for the crime. The cove west of Wilder Beach came to be known as the Old Russian Cove or Smugglers Cove. In spite of all of his ventures, financial difficulties began to surface, and Bolcoff was forced to sell the rancho to Moses Meder. After this, little is known of Bolcoff or his activities.

MOSES A. MEDER

Moses Meder acquired Bolcoff's property in 1854. He constructed several buildings on the ranch, many of which are still standing. These structures included a creamery, at least one granary, a blacksmith shop and an equipment and wagon shed.

Born in 1802 in Ellsworth, New Hampshire, Moses grew up in a tiny town of about forty residents. In 1846, he sailed with his wife, Sarah, and daughter, Angeline, from New York to San Francisco on the steamship *Brooklyn*. The vessel took six months to sail around Cape Horn, surviving two terrible storms. Moses's family was part of a group of Latter-day Saints who had gathered together to make their way west by pooling their money and chartering a ship.

"Small and well-worn, the 450-ton Brooklyn was a typical three-masted, full-rigged Yankee trading ship. The 2,500 square feet of cramped space between decks became the living quarters for families, with a long table, backless benches and sleeping bunks all bolted to the deck," one story revealed. "In the low-ceiling area, only children could stand upright. Below, crammed into the hold, were water barrels, crates of chickens, two cows, forty pigs, two sawmills, a gristmill, tools for 800 farmers, a printing press and much more of everything they thought would be needed to establish a new home."

The following year, Moses moved his family to Santa Cruz, where he made a living by building lumber mills and giving small loans on properties. In the late 1850s, Moses constructed a new home on the rancho, now the front portion of the old farmhouse. He continued many of the ranching and farming activities formerly carried on by his predecessor. He also expanded operations, building a creamery and a dairy barn.

"Few dairy farms provided winter protection for their cattle until the 1860s when the cow barn came into wide use," one historian revealed. "Most cows, however, continued to be herded into paddocks or corrals to be milked twice a day and were brought indoors only in inclement weather."

By 1860, Moses's holdings encompassed numerous farm implements and machinery, horses, pigs, milk cows and other cattle, hundreds of bushels of wheat, barley and hay and hundreds of pounds of cheese and butter. The butter he produced sold for one dollar a pound in San Francisco, expensive for the time.

Moses passed away in 1890 at the age of eighty-eight, "having been in feeble health for many months." At that time, he had experienced the painful loss of his wife, age sixty-seven, in 1872 and his daughter, just twenty-five, in 1860. Hopefully, he was comforted by the knowledge that he had provided well for them, "had been handy at many things" and had achieved the status of a wealthy entrepreneur in lumber, petroleum and real estate. Numerous locations around Santa Cruz still bear his name.

LEVI K. BALDWIN

Deloss Wilder's former business partner, Levi K. Baldwin, was born in 1820 in Egremont, Massachusetts. Located on the western edge of the state, the area was described as "mostly lightly settled forests and farmland." Levi married Emeline Parsons in 1843 and raised a daughter. For many years, Levi operated a successful farm. Unluckily, he lost most of his hard-earned money due to poor investments. In 1858, the family left for California, settling in Marin County near his uncle's ranch.

Levi's uncle Zadock Karner ventured to San Francisco in 1851 on the first voyage of the steamer *Golden Gate* via the Isthmus of Panama. In his native Massachusetts, he was a farmer, grocer and jeweler. While at the California mines, he operated a hotel for six years and worked as a watchmaker. Later, he purchased a ranch in Olema Valley in rural west Marin to establish a dairy and butter business.

Levi and his family occupied a house on the site of the prosperous Truttman Ranch. By 1860, the thriving Karner and Baldwin dairy, known as L.K. Baldwin & Co., supported seventy milk cows, which produced thousands of pounds of butter. Four hired hands performed general farm work, milking and raising wheat, oats, barley and hay. One of the farmhands was Emeline Baldwin's brother Charles Parsons, who five years later would develop another early dairy ranch to the south.

In early 1862, a correspondent from the *California Farmer* visited the Olema Valley ranches. In glowing terms, he singled out Baldwin's dairy as the best and most successful in the area. In the opinion of the writer, "Karner and Baldwin's may be called a Real Dairy Ranch. It embraces 550 acres, 250 head of stock and 100 milkers. The success of this dairy should stimulate everyone in the dairy business."

The correspondent concluded by saying: "We do love to praise well doing. We admire to see animals well cared for, neatness and cleanliness in a dairy and yet upon a little reflection, all men of good common sense, men that love their business, know their own interest is best promoted by such means. Therefore, having enjoyed the courtesy and hospitality of the proprietors of this ranch, we will say, that they have manifested a large share of wisdom and sound common sense, added to judgement and knowledge, in the management of their dairy business, which is in most prosperous condition."

By 1867, Levi owned the former properties of Stephen Barnaby, Zadock Karner and William Johnson, totaling 1,004 acres. Because his "sound judgement and business abilities were recognized by his neighbors," he served for three terms on the Marin County Board of Supervisors.

In 1871, Levi and Deloss Wilder purchased over four thousand acres of the former Rancho del Refugio. The following year, he moved his family to Santa Cruz, where they built a new creamery on the property. Levi passed away in 1904 in his beloved Santa Cruz.

DELOSS D. WILDER

Deloss Wilder was born in West Hartland, Connecticut, in 1826. He was raised on a farm where it was difficult to sustain a living. According to one biographer, "It required the greatest exertion and the most rigid economy to make ends meet."

At the age of ten, he worked as a farm laborer for $6.50 a month, taking half of his pay in store orders. Six years later, he managed to save enough money to start a book agency in Ohio. When the business failed to thrive, he bought a horse and saddle and started back to his Connecticut home.

Unfortunately, he miscalculated the severity of the weather, facing temperatures of fifteen degrees below zero. His health began to fail, but he was able to find his way to relatives in New York. He remained there for some time, recuperated and found a job building stone fences. The work enabled him to earn about one dollar a day.

In 1853, Deloss left for California, arriving in Stockton after a seven-month journey across the country. Like so many of those who trekked to California in the early 1850s, his first efforts were in the gold mines. He went on to Marin in 1859 with a sum of about $200. It was just enough to start a chicken ranch and a small dairy. Meeting with some success, Deloss married Miranda Finch in 1867, and they raised two sons, Deloss Burton and Melvin Dwight.

The family moved on to Santa Cruz in 1871, when Deloss partnered with Levi Baldwin. In 1875, Levi registered his butter trademark with the secretary of state. The butter was in considerable demand at San Francisco's bustling Washington Market, always commanding the highest prices.

In spite of acquiring an enviable reputation for making quality butter, the partnership dissolved in 1885. Levi and Deloss parted amicably, splitting the ranch acreage between them. Levi acquired the upper portion of the ranch; Deloss secured the lower portion on Meder Creek, which includes the present state park cultural preserve area, for $32,000.

INNOVATIONS ON THE RANCH

Deloss continued to build on what he began with Levi. Around 1886, Deloss bought two Pelton waterwheels. Lester Pelton invented the wheel during the gold rush. At the time, there was a huge demand for new power sources to run the machinery and the lumber mills necessary to expand the mines. The steam engine was a popular source of power, but it used massive amounts of coal and wood that devastated area forests. Fast-moving creeks and waterfalls were identified as an untapped and abundant source of power.

The Pelton wheel was uniquely suited to California's smaller waterways. It ran on the force of the movement of water rather than on its volume. As

Opposite: Lester Pelton was an American inventor who contributed to the development of hydroelectricity and hydropower during the California Gold Rush. *National Museum of American History*.

Right: Deloss Wilder innovated his dairy ranch with a Pelton waterwheel, which extracts energy from the impulse of moving water. *National Museum of American History*.

long as there was a small creek or stream that moved quickly, energy could be extracted from it by using the wheel.

Deloss also built a reservoir on a hilltop some 9,000 feet from the farm complex in order to take advantage of the 216-foot drop in elevation. He used an eight-inch pipe full of rushing water to feed the wheels, producing one hundred horsepower. A San Francisco newspaper credited Wilder with inventing "artificial sunrise" by bringing electricity to the ranch.

By 1890, a forge and generators were also powered by water. It also ran a lathe, a sander, a drill press and even a coffee grinder (a necessity when you're up before dawn to milk cows). Other Pelton wheels around the property, positioned along a network of pipes, ran a table saw and the cream separator. This innovative use of the waterwheel revolutionized the dairy industry and the local economy. Wilder Ranch was the only ranch in the area in the 1890s that had electricity, and it was a beacon for miles. A new Victorian farmhouse was built in 1897.

Deloss was described in the following way: "Despite his many years, with hair and beard as white as those of a patriarch, he still actively superintends and personally manages his extensive interests and exhibits an industry and an energy that would not only be a credit to any young man but would insure his prosperity."

When Deloss passed away on his ranch at age eighty in 1906, he had risen to become one of the most successful dairymen in the county. His butter was much sought after, and he had a long-standing order from a firm in San Francisco for all that he could produce. He had also gained an enviable reputation. "He was a man generous and hospitable," one writer stated. "Good natured and honorable in every business transaction, he has always been spoken of most highly by neighbors and others with whom he came in contact."

The improvements made by the owners on what is now Wilder Ranch made major contributions to the dairy and farming industries. The Wilder family continued to work the land until 1969, when the ranch's income could no longer sustain it. In the 1970s, the land was proposed for a housing development, but local citizens blocked the project. In 1974, California State Parks acquired the property to preserve its natural environment and cultural history. Today, the ranch reflects the unique features added by its colorful pioneering residents, each of whom left a distinct imprint.

II

HENRY COWELL REDWOODS STATE PARK

HENRY COWELL, LIME BARON

Henry Cowell Redwoods State Park in Felton, seven miles northeast of Santa Cruz, offers both spectacular scenery and historical significance. The story of Cowell Ranch cannot be told without highlighting the area's shipping and lime trade. The trade expanded and excelled not only by the endeavors of Henry Cowell, but also by those of Isaac Davis and Albion Jordan. All were truly self-made men.

VALUABLE LIME

The rich soil of California offers many valuable products. One of the most important is lime. While it's found in various parts of California, it is especially prevalent in Santa Cruz. In the 1830s and 1840s, construction of brick buildings became more prevalent. As a result, the use of lime increased.

Lime was the essential ingredient in the mortar that held the bricks together and in the plaster that often covered the interior walls. Lime was also used to make whitewash, a much cheaper alternative to paint. By the 1850s, lime was a valuable product with other uses, such as leather tanning and soapmaking.

Lime was made by heating limestone to two thousand degrees in stone kilns. Both the ancient Egyptians and the Romans used the process, and the Spanish brought the technology to California, building kilns at several of their missions. Early kiln workers in Santa Cruz used redwood trees as fuel for the kilns. It took two days to load the lumps of limestone into the kiln and five days to fire them completely. Then, it took two days to let the lime cool and two more days to unload. The product created in the kiln was a powdery substance called quicklime. Each cycle created approximately one thousand barrels of lime, which would then be shipped to San Francisco.

Barrel makers, known as coopers, built redwood barrels that were used to pack and ship lime. Timber staves were usually heated or steamed to make them pliable. Barrel hoops were added to hold the wood slats in place. Originally, hoops were made from flexible hazelnut wands. Later, steel hoops were used.

Once the barrels were filled with lime from the kilns, they were stored in a building called a cooperage. They were then loaded onto wagons and taken to the wharf for shipment. Each barrel contained 150 pounds of lime.

SELF-RELIANT AND AMBITIOUS

Albion Jordan started a lime business with Isaac Davis in 1853. It was the first in Santa Cruz. *Santa Cruz Museum of Art & History.*

The first commercial-scale manufacturer of lime in Santa Cruz was the Davis-Jordan Lime Company. Isaac E. Davis and Albion P. Jordan shared much in common. Each spent his early life in New England. Born in Massachusetts in 1823, Isaac grew up in a large farming family. Little else is known about that period except that he lost both parents early in life.

Albion entered the world in 1826, the son of Captain Peter Jordan of Brunswick, Maine. The enterprising town became a major producer of lumber, with as many as two dozen sawmills. Some of the lumber went into shipbuilding. Other firms produced paper, soap, flour, marble and granite work, carriages and harnesses, plows, furniture, shoes, even confections. It was also the site of the first cotton mill in Maine, established to make yarn.

Each acquired a good education and gained a practical knowledge of engineering. The two were self-reliant and ambitious. Both men traveled to California in 1849 in search of gold. Soon, each determined that toiling in the gritty mines was not the way to find a better life. Somehow, each man made his way aboard a steamer plying the Sacramento River. It was there that they met. Isaac was the fireman on the vessel, and Albion was the ship's engineer. In 1851, they joined in partnership to run a steamship between San Francisco and Stockton.

Some of Northern California's earliest steamboats operated on the popular Sacramento and San Joaquin Rivers between San Francisco, Sacramento and Stockton. According to one steamboat authority, "After the first discovery of gold in California the first shipping on the bays and up the rivers were by ocean going craft that were able to sail close to the wind and of a shallow enough draft to be able to sail up the river channels and sloughs. Regular service up the rivers was provided primarily by schooners and launches to Sacramento and Stockton, often taking a week or more to make the trip."

Observing sprouting towns and burgeoning building industries, the men were perceptive enough to create their own enterprise in limestone. The Davis-Jordan Lime Company prospered beyond their expectations. Between 1853 and 1865, the firm was the major lime manufacturer in Santa Cruz.

The *Daily Alta* reported in 1855: "As the construction of fine brick buildings here and in Sacramento and Marysville became more general, the use of lime has increased so that from Santa Cruz alone, not counting other quarries in the State, about 700 barrels a week have been brought. The lime is of such excellent quality. Last year one company, Davis & Jordan, got out 35,000 barrels, all of which was shipped to San Francisco."

Isaac and Albion chose the location for their business carefully. The region held an abundance of limestone and endless forests of trees to cut and burn in processing lime. It was also located close to the sea. The partners built and operated a wharf for shipping lime and purchased a small fleet of schooners to deliver their product to San Francisco.

STALWART SCHOONER CAPTAIN

An important component of the lime trade is the way in which it was transported to various markets. Schooners sailed unceasingly along the Pacific coast, hustling from port to port. These agile little ships hauled hundreds of tons of goods each year in all kinds of weather. One of the many schooner skippers who plied coastal waters was Captain Timothy Herbert Dame.

Timothy was born in New Hampshire in the mid-1820s. He enlisted in the U.S. Navy to serve during the Mexican-American War. He mustered onto the USS *Ohio* in Boston in late 1846 and was discharged from service in 1849. Like throngs of other fortune seekers, he journeyed to California in search of gold.

Before long, he returned to the sea, captaining the schooners *Mount Vernon* and *Queen of the West* for the Davis-Jordan Lime Company. His route was primarily between Santa Cruz and San Francisco. Carrying cargoes of lime can be a dangerous venture. If not handled properly, lime can become wet and burst into flames, endangering a ship and its crew.

Fortunately, Timothy had a sterling record as a ship's master. According to one local newspaper, "Not a more careful commander, or one better acquainted with the coast than Captain Dame, can scarcely be found on the Pacific."

In 1857, Timothy ushered in a new era in Santa Cruz as captain of the new steamer *Santa Cruz* for Davis-Jordan. This ship reduced travel time between Santa Cruz and San Francisco from what could be thirty or more hours to seven or eight.

COWELL TAKES OVER

On March 4, 1859, Albion and Mary Elizabeth Perry were married. He had built a house near the lime kilns, and it was there that they raised their family. Sadly, by early 1865, Albion was dying from tuberculosis and decided to sell his half of the business. Earlier, Henry Cowell had made a substantial loan to Isaac and Albion's business and was the first potential buyer they approached. "Mr. Jordan was very unwell at the time, and the papers were made out in haste for fear that he would not live to sign the deeds," Henry said later. "I surrendered a note against Davis and Jordan for $22,000 and a little over, gave them $15,000 in cash, and my note for $25,000 to be paid in two years, and half of it to be paid in one year."

Albion passed away in November 1866 at the early age of forty. One newspaper remembered him as "universally loved by those sustaining business relations with him. He was a noble and warm friend, always pleasant and quick with a word from the heart."

Their enterprise would continue on as the Davis-Cowell Lime Company. Without hesitation, Henry moved his family to Santa Cruz and took on supervising operations. He declared, "I was cutting wood, hauling it, getting out rock and burning it into lime, making lime barrels and shipping them."

Above: Part of a Henry Cowell & Company receipt lists some of the diverse products sold by the firm. *Friends of Cowell Lime Works.*

Left: A bird's-eye view of Santa Cruz shows the Davis-Jordan wharf on the far left. Docked schooners await loading. *G.B. Gifford.*

Interestingly, Henry was another New Englander. He was born in 1819 on a farm in Wrentham, Massachusetts, about twenty-seven miles southwest of Boston. The area was described as "a good old farming town with two mills for crude woolen goods and four or five saw and grist mills." As the town grew, other industries followed, including boat building, boot manufacturing, jewelry fabrication and carriage assembly.

Henry was the youngest of eleven children. He and his older brother John were lured to California by the gold rush. Rather than digging in the mines, one writer pointed out, "they used their brains, not their brawn." They survived by selling goods to miners, acting as agents for eastern merchants. By 1850, they had begun operating a hauling and storing business in San Francisco. Initially, John managed the enterprise. In 1854, after Henry married his sweetheart, Harriet Elizabeth Carpenter, he became the manager of the drayage firm. In 1860, John fell ill and sold his interests to Henry.

By 1886, Henry was reported to have the highest income in Santa Cruz County. In addition to owning ten thousand acres of land in the area, his businesses included limestone quarries, shipping, logging, cattle, cement trade and large landholdings, ranches and lime deposits in fifteen counties.

When Isaac Davis died in 1888, newspapers extolled him as a "most excellent man and good citizen." According to one report, "He was a very retiring man, but public-spirited to an unusual degree, and while he declined honors for himself, was always working to secure the advancement of his city and associates. When his type of citizen has passed away, the city and state still have need of these men of iron who, undaunted by obstacles, forged their way to the front through their own initiative, good judgment and broad vision."

Henry purchased the remainder of the lime company for $400,000. The firm's name changed again, this time to the Henry Cowell Lime and Cement Company. It had become a large enterprise employing 175 men with an annual payroll of $100,000. A peculiarity of the company was its payday. It came only once a year, when the men were paid with gold coins.

When Isaac Davis died in 1888, Henry Cowell bought and renamed the firm the Henry Cowell Lime and Cement Company. *Friends of Cowell Lime Works.*

"The principal manufacturer of lime in this county is Henry Cowell. The products of his kilns constitute a considerable part of the exports of this county. It is scarcely hyperbolical to say that the supply of limestone in this county is inexhaustible, as there is enough here to supply the world for the next century," a state trade journal asserted. "This industry gives employment to several hundred men, not less than a hundred being in the employ of Mr. Cowell. Great ox teams are used to haul fuel from the woods. He owns a warehouse in Santa Cruz with a connecting wharf which ships by schooner the products of his kilns."

DIVERSE INTERESTS

Henry and his family lived in the Albion Jordan home. It was, indeed, an honor to do so, for Albion was well liked in Santa Cruz and worked for the betterment of the young town. "He was generous, perhaps a little too generous, in making company resources available to the community," author and lime expert Frank Perry reflected. "Cowell, on the other hand, was all business. Cowell sometimes fought against improvements for the community as a whole, such as new roads or railroads, because they would have benefited competing lime companies. During the late 1860s and 1870s these actions spawned a growing dislike and distrust of Henry Cowell among many Santa Cruzans."

In 1897, Henry moved his family to a San Francisco mansion. Although sometimes dubbed a "lime baron," he had diverse business interests. These included raising cattle and other livestock, farming, buying and selling property and water rights, making loans and more.

Henry's business interests even extended to Alaska. He sat on the board of directors of the North American Commercial Company, which in 1890 secured an exclusive twenty-year lease from the federal government for the taking of fur seals on the islands of St. Paul and St. George. It was estimated that the company would be harvesting one hundred thousand pelts per year.

Henry had ranches scattered across much of Northern and Central California, from the Pacific shore to the Sierra foothills. According to early newspaper accounts, many were apparently acquired through foreclosures.

With his many business interests came disputes. In March 1903, Henry bought a two-thousand-acre ranch on the Merced River. He and a neighbor, Daniel Ingalsbe, argued over the boundary line. Daniel claimed that some of Henry's cattle destroyed his family's corn crop and demanded payment of $500. Henry refused. When he later visited his landholdings in Merced, Ingalsbe's son Leigh continued the argument with a revolver.

Henry was shot in the shoulder. Although the wound was called "minor" by the authorities, he suffered a severe loss of blood. He said that he never felt the same after the incident. Leigh was found to be violently insane at the time of the shooting and was acquitted. Henry died on August 4, 1903. He was eighty-four years old and worth $3 million (almost $100 million in today's terms).

"Henry Cowell had a powerful physical frame, a vigorous intellect and an indomitable will," an obituary in the *Santa Cruz Surf* declared. "He willed to be a rich man and he succeeded. Such men cannot be kept down."

CHARITABLE ACTS

Henry's five children inherited his estate. His surviving two daughters and two sons were generous community donors. Ernest Cowell set up a scholarship fund at Santa Cruz High School. He also aided the Santa Cruz Free Library. Sisters Helen and Isabelle frequently donated to hospitals and to relief funds for victims of various disasters. Ultimately, nearly the entire Cowell family fortune went to charity.

Samuel Henry Cowell (called S.H. or Harry), who was the last surviving heir, established the S.H. Cowell Foundation. One of his last acts of generosity was to donate part of his sprawling land on the condition that a park be named for his father. On August 18, 1954, Henry Cowell Redwoods State Park was formally dedicated as a new unit in the California State Parks system.

Harry died in February 1955 at the age of ninety-three. "The death of Harry Cowell brings to an end one of California's foremost families, owners of great properties and, through their philanthropy, benefactors of thousands of students and residents of the state where they obtained their wealth," the *Santa Cruz Sentinel* observed. "Henry Cowell Redwoods State Park will remain a perpetual monument, not only to Henry Cowell, but to Harry Cowell."

Elements of Cowell Ranch that still remain include barns, a blacksmith shop, a ranch house, a cookhouse and workers' cabins. In addition, a thirty-two-acre Cowell Lime Works Historic District is located nearby within the University of California, Santa Cruz. In addition to four lime kilns, a cooperage and other features relating to lime manufacture, the historic district includes other structures associated with Cowell Ranch. The district was listed in the National Register of Historic Places in 2007. Taken together, it is an absorbing step back into the beginnings of California and one of its most important industries.

SEACLIFF STATE BEACH

WILLIAM LESLIE COMYN, VISIONARY SHIPBUILDER

Seacliff is situated about seven miles southeast of Santa Cruz. Before the 1920s, the area was used for pasture and sugar beet production. In the years since, it has been known as the site of the distinctive concrete ship SS *Palo Alto*. The vessel was crafted by the visionary shipbuilder and businessman William Leslie Comyn.

EARLY CONCRETE SHIPS

The first concrete vessel was a rowboat crafted in 1848 by Joseph Louis Lambot in southern France. Born in 1814, Lambot studied in Paris, where his uncle Baron Lambot was aide-de-camp to the Duke of Bourbon. He constructed a series of rowboats using a procedure he called "Fericement." The process was the forerunner of what we know today as ferro-cement. He used steel rods to form a wire mesh that created a skeleton of the ship's hull. Concrete was poured over the form to shape the hull.

"My invention is a new product that can replace timber (in wood flooring, water containers, plant pots, etc.) that is exposed to damage by water or dampness," he stated. "The base for the new substance is a metal net of wire, or rods interconnected to form a flexible woven mat."

The prototype was presented at the 1855 World's Fair (Exposition Universelle) in Paris. Although Lambot's rowboat later sank, it was preserved in anaerobic mud at the bottom of a lake. The boat was recovered more than one hundred years later and is preserved at the Museum of Brignoles. Lambot died in Brignoles in 1887.

The first practical seagoing ship of concrete was the eighty-four-foot motorship *Namsenfjord*, which was designed and built by Norwegian shipbuilder Nicolay Knudtzon Fougner and his brother Hermann. Based on a 1912 patent, they began with the construction of concrete barges called lighters. The *Namsenfjord* was completed in 1917 and approved by classification societies that same year.

According to Nicolay, "Concrete ships are cheaper to build and cost less in upkeep. They are less subject to vibration from engines and, owing to the heavier hull, they require less ballast when running light and have easier movements in rough seas. Concrete ships are more quickly and more cheaply repaired. They are fireproof and not subject to corrosion. They have better insulating properties for cargoes, such as ice, fruit, etc., and are more easily kept clean."

Not much is known of him. He was born in Norway in December 1884 and attended Trondheim Technical College, now Norwegian University of Science and Technology, in 1906. He worked in New York and Detroit, Michigan, as an engineer and representative for the Trussed Concrete Steel Company of America.

Imagination and Curiosity

William Leslie Comyn produced the first concrete ship in America. Born in London, England, in 1877, he was always filled with vision, imagination and curiosity. His family had a noted history. His father, Charles, was an English civil servant. His great-uncle Stephen George Comyn had been naval chaplain to the famous English admiral Lord Horatio Nelson.

Leslie, as he preferred to be called, was educated at select boarding schools. On graduation, he founded a shipping company called Comyn, Singleton and Dunn. Through this enterprise, he journeyed to California, where he settled and became a businessman in San Francisco. He married Ann Gerber, and together they raised three children.

By the early 1900s, the size and cost of merchant vessels had increased significantly. Leslie recognized "the futility of building wooden ships from green lumber and the general lack of shipyard proximity to steel plants." He proposed creating vessels with concrete hulls to the newly formed U.S. Shipping Board but found little interest.

Left: During World War I, the U.S. Shipping Board created the Emergency Fleet Corporation to oversee production of the nation's ships. *U.S. Shipping Board*.

Below: The SS *Faith*, the first concrete ship built in America, was constructed by William Comyn at his shipbuilding company in Oakland, California. *Captain James McNamara*.

Despite the indifference, he was convinced of the practicality, durability and versatility of concrete vessels. While he waited for government officials to warm to the idea, he took the initiative to build ferro-cement ships on his own. He knew the right moment would come. Leslie formed the San Francisco Ship Building Company in Redwood City, a port town during the gold rush that became the county seat of newly formed San Mateo County in 1856.

He hired the prominent Alan MacDonald of MacDonald & Kahn, construction managers, and civil engineer Victor H. Poss to design a concrete ship. In September 1917, they began construction on a 6,125-ton steamer. Triple-expansion engines would power the ship to ten knots. On March 18, 1918, the SS *Faith* was launched at a cost of $750,000. Experts who witnessed the launch predicted that concrete construction would mark a new era in shipbuilding. They acknowledged that utility rather than speed was expressed in the concrete ship's lines, somewhat as if it "might be carved out of rock, so massive was her build." No doubt, it could stand the stresses of sea duty.

Leslie had something to say as well. "When the first steel vessels were built, people said they would not float, or if they did, they would be too heavy to be serviceable. Now, they say the same thing about concrete," he smirked a bit. "But all the engineers we have taken over this boat, including many who said it was an impossible undertaking, now agree that it is a success. The lie is given to the theory that stone won't float."

The *Faith* left San Francisco on May 22 on its first commercial voyage with a cargo of rock salt and copper ore assigned to Seattle. It traded in the eastern Pacific, Caribbean and North Atlantic until December 1921. The vessel was then sold and used as a breakwater in Cuba before being broken up in 1926.

Leslie must have felt particularly acknowledged in June 1919. His pioneering work was recognized with a special medal from the American Concrete Institute. "Faith is a quality which we are told will move mountains. In the development of reinforced concrete, it is the men of faith who pushed ahead early construction in advance of theory, codes or formulations," W.K. Hatt, president of the institute, reflected. "We honor the achievements of W. Leslie Comyn, who, while others were thinking and talking of the difficulties and dangers of building and launching a concrete ship, assembled a group of men and constructed a concrete ship, the *Faith*."

World War I

America's growing involvement in World War I began after German submarines relentlessly attacked U.S. merchant ships. On April 6, 1916, President Woodrow Wilson asked Congress to declare war on Germany. A month later, he also requested the formation of the U.S. Shipping Board to oversee the nation's wartime production activities.

The board formed the Emergency Fleet Corporation for the "purchase, construction, equipment, lease, charter, maintenance and operation of merchant vessels in the commerce of the United States." It engaged in what was then the greatest construction task ever attempted by a single organization.

"Our country needs ships to carry our boys 'over there' and keep them well supplied with food, clothing, and the munitions of war," one factory poster declared. "The ships can be completed only as fast as the material and equipment for each ship arrives in the shipyard. If every man does a better day's work every day, the ships can be built faster."

By 1918, steel shortages created a demand for alternate shipbuilding materials. The shipping board embarked on an $8 billion shipbuilding program using concrete. Concrete ships became important to the war effort, because a hull made of concrete required about a third less steel per ton than a ship made of steel.

Interestingly, the U.S. government turned to Nicolay Fougner, engaging him to consult with the Emergency Fleet Corporation program to help build concrete ships. He formed the Fougner Company with his brother Hermann, but at some point the firm went bankrupt. He traveled to Argentina and then back to America, sharing his knowledge of shipbuilding in the form of a book, *Seagoing and Other Concrete Ships*. Further records for him do not seem to exist after 1942.

Meanwhile, the board authorized a fleet of thirty-eight concrete ships for the war effort. The vessels would be used for transport purposes, mainly as steamers and oil tankers. They were built at shipyards in New York, Georgia, North Carolina, Alabama, Florida and California. Only twelve concrete ships were completed. Unfortunately, none of them saw combat.

The SS *Palo Alto*

One of the ships built during the war was the oil tanker SS *Palo Alto*. The vessel was constructed by Leslie Comyn's San Francisco Shipbuilding

Company at the U.S. Naval Shipyard in Oakland, twelve miles across the bay. The cement used for building the *Palo Alto*'s thin concrete hull came from Davenport, just north of Santa Cruz. It is thought that some of the brick used in place of gravel to lighten the weight was rubble from the San Francisco earthquake. It was equipped with a 2,800-horsepower steam engine, a bronze propeller, white Norwegian ash decks and fourteen compartments to hold three million gallons of oil.

The ship was launched in May 1918, just six months before the armistice was signed ending World War I. As a result, the *Palo Alto* sat idle at the Suisun Bay Reserve Fleet in Benicia, about thirty-five miles north of San Francisco. In November 1924, it was sold to the Oliver J. Colson Company for oil storage, then to Oakland machinery dealer R.C. Porter. In 1929, the vessel was purchased by a Nevada-based company called Seacliff Amusement Corporation. Its intention was to create "a most unique amusement enterprise."

Picturing the *Palo Alto* as an excellent location for fun and fishing, the company had it towed to Seacliff Beach. A 630-foot pier was built to connect with the ship's stern. The vessel was sunk a few feet into the water so the keel could rest firmly on the ocean's sandy bottom. It was then refitted to accommodate a casino, a dance hall, a heated swimming pool and a restaurant.

In the summer of 1930, over three thousand people attended the ship's grand opening, which boasted "amusements galore." The Fish Palace was hailed as "the finest seafood restaurant on the Pacific Coast." The Rainbow Ballroom featured famous big band acts like Paul Whiteman, Benny Goodman and Tommy Dorsey. The ship was also a hot spot for games of chance. There were slot machines and bingo on the deck and, it's

The SS *Palo Alto* was a World War I concrete ship. Never used in combat, it became Seacliff's amusement vessel. *Naval History and Heritage Command.*

rumored, gambling below. Prohibition was in effect, but the ship never ran short of alcohol. Bootleg whiskey was delivered directly onto the ship by rumrunners. Apparently, the surrounding beach was a notorious landing for delivering illegal liquor.

The attraction became extremely successful but lasted a mere two years. The seasonality of the business and the Great Depression affected operations, leaving Seacliff Amusement Corporation no alternative but to declare bankruptcy.

Not long after the company's demise, a winter storm ravaged the area, and the *Palo Alto* was left with a huge crack in its midsection. After the ship was further damaged by the sea, the bankrupted owners stripped the vessel of all of its valuable parts, taking the steel, the engines and even the dance floor. Somehow, a local resident managed to salvage the ship's running lights and donated them to the Seacliff State Beach visitor center.

A Pier and Artificial Reef

In 1936, the State of California purchased the ship for $1. Its original estimated cost was $1.5 million. The vessel was converted into a fishing pier, which immediately became popular with local anglers. The *Palo Alto* also became an official part of Seacliff State Beach.

In 1946, William Leslie Comyn passed away, knowing that his unique ship lived on. He sold San Francisco Shipbuilding Company in 1919 to the French-American Steamship Lines. He went on to establish other shipping and import-export enterprises, including W.L. Comyn & Company, followed by W.L. Comyn & Sons. He and his wife are buried at East Lawn Memorial Park in Sacramento.

The *Palo Alto* became a favorite visiting spot for fishermen and curiosity seekers alike. In 1950, portions of the vessel became unsafe and were closed. Over time, the ship's condition worsened due to constant exposure to storms. A restoration project that took place between 1983 and 1988 saw the ship open once again as a recreational spot. However, a permanent visitor ban was imposed on the *Palo Alto* in 1998.

In 2003, oil leaking from an unknown source resulted in dozens of seabird fatalities. In early 2005, the leak was traced to the *Palo Alto*. In the fall of 2006, the California Department of Fish and Wildlife began a cleanup project during which workers pumped five hundred gallons of oil from the vessel.

The ship continues to deteriorate, and each storm sees it breaking apart a little more. In 2016, strong waves turned one of the pieces over to its side. In January 2017, the stern was torn off. Today, the ship serves as an artificial reef for seabirds and underwater life.

In 2019, local organizations joined together to hold a centennial celebration for the SS *Palo Alto*, "the most famous concrete ship on the West Coast." Despite its inevitable decline, Seacliff's unique nautical relic still holds significant historical and sentimental value. In time, it may slip farther beneath the water, even disappear, but memories of it will always remain.

EPILOGUE

Coastside Rumrunners

Throughout this book, you have discovered the intrepid people who developed industries such as lumber, lime, dairies, even general stores up and down the Coastside. One industry that is found in the shadows of the coast is rum-running and, by extension, speakeasies.

The numerous isolated nooks and crannies of the Coastside and the many small dog hole ports made perfect landing sites, secret and secluded, for bringing ashore illegal liquor. According to one state park ranger, "There was alcohol hidden everywhere."

Throughout the 1920s, when Prohibition was in full swing, the flow of liquor from the sea was unprecedented. By far the most famous period of rum-running occurred in the United States between 1920 and 1933. The passing of the Eighteenth Amendment prohibited the sale, possession and consumption of alcohol. It proved to be an extremely unpopular law. Reveling in an otherwise liberated era, many citizens enjoyed a good, stiff drink now and again, even if it was illegal.

A Florida boatbuilder and excursion boat captain named Bill McCoy, who became the self-styled "King of the Rum Runners," set the pattern for smuggling liquor by sea. He brought ships to the edge of the three-mile limit of U.S. jurisdiction and sold his wares to "contact boats" owned by local fishermen and small-boat captains. McCoy was famous for never watering his booze and selling only top-of-the-line name brands. Reputedly, this was the origin of the term the "Real McCoy," meaning genuine and on the level.

As the demand for forbidden liquor grew, so did the enticements of rum-running. Soon, the idea caught on with hundreds of other boat owners along the country's coastlines. For many, it was the only way to make a living. "I was in the rum running business for a couple of years," one skipper admitted. "It was the only dollar you could make."

The three-mile limit became known as the "Rum Line," and vessels waiting to receive illegal spirits were called "Rum Row." In 1924, the Rum Line was extended to a twelve-mile limit, making it more difficult for smaller and less seaworthy craft to travel the distance. With the run to shore longer, chances of detection increased. In a desperate attempt to avoid arrest, some rumrunners dumped their cargo, set the vessel on fire and abandoned ship.

Often, crews armed themselves against government ships and against other rumrunners. Some rum boats sank others to hijack precious cargo rather than journey to Canada or Mexico to restock their liquid supplies. At night, even in fog, they often ran at high speeds and without lights. Many smashed into rocks, spilling their profits overboard.

Ironically, one thing that rumrunners seldom carried was rum. The name was a holdover from the rum smuggling of colonial days and from the habit of referring to all liquor as the "demon rum." Most of the cargo was whiskey-bottled in Canada and Mexico by professional distillers.

In addition to rum-running operations, the isolated Coastside was also dotted with small distilleries run by bootleggers. The openness of the countryside, usually void of traffic, made it nearly impossible for officials to pounce on bootleggers by surprise. Booze was stored in barns, fields or in coastal coves until it could be safely transported to the cities in cars or trucks, often driven by women.

In towns all over the coast, hotels, restaurants, roadhouses, wharves, farms and factories were used for clandestine operations. Hooch was camouflaged in the secret recesses of specially made cabinetry or in hen houses and chicken coops. Liquor was often concealed in laundry bags, disguised among produce as vegetables or stowed in sacks of coal. A number of locations not only produced illegal goods but also promoted illicit services. As the daughter of one proprietor explained, "There was a lot of hanky-panky going on."

Along California's colorful Coastside, there are stories everywhere you go. All you have to do is ask any park ranger.

BIBLIOGRAPHY

1. McNee Ranch State Park

Alameda (CA) Sun. "Historic Surveyor Once Lived in Island City." June 20, 2019.

California State Parks. "Montara Mountain Walk." August 8, 2015.

Carle, David. *Putting California on the Map: Von Schmidt's Line.* Lee Vining, CA: Phalarope Press, 2018.

Chief of Engineers Annual Report. Washington, DC: Government Printing Office, 1887.

Eastern Sierra History Journal. "Putting California on the Map: Von Schmidt's Lines." 2020.

Engineering and Building Record. "Building Construction Details." June–November 1887.

Executive Documents of the House of Representatives. Washington, DC: Government Printing Office, 1889.

"Ghost Rails." KCET, September 8, 2016.

Half Moon Bay (CA) Review. "A Magnificent Failure." March 15, 2012.

Report of the Secretary of the Navy. Washington, DC: Government Printing Office, 1886.

San Jose Mercury News. "Ghostly Ruins of WWII Bunker." November 23, 2013.

San Mateo Coast Sector Volunteer Study Guide. "McNee Ranch History." January 2009.

Santa Rosa (CA) Press Democrat. "Duncan McNee Passes Away." January 21, 1913.

Smallfield, W.E., and Robert Campbell. *The Story of Renfrew.* Ontario, CA: Renfrew, Smallfield & Son, 1919.

Uzes, Francois. *Chaining the Land: A History of Surveying in California.* Sacramento, CA: Landmark Enterprise, 1977.

Vander Werf, Barbara. *Montara Mountain.* El Granada, CA: Gum Tree Lane Books, 1994.

2. Burleigh H. Murray Ranch State Park

Alexander, Philip, and Charles Hamm. *History of San Mateo County.* Burlingame, CA: Burlingame Publishing Company, 1916.

Burleigh Murray Historic Structures Report. California Department of Parks and Recreation. June 26, 1987.

Cloud, Roy. *History of San Mateo County.* Chicago: S.J. Clarke Publishing, 1928.

Gualtieri, Kathryn. *Half Moon Bay: Birth of a Coastside Town.* Half Moon Bay, CA: Spanishtown Historical Society, 1988.

Historic Resources Inventory of Mills Barn, Mills Home and Mills Ranch. California Department of Parks and Recreation. September 26, 1982.

Historic Resources Inventory of Mills Creek Ranch. California Department of Parks and Recreation. November 1983.

Letter to Director of California Parks and Recreation from State Historic Preservation Officer regarding placement of Robert Mills Dairy Barn on National Register of Historic Places. April 4, 1990. Office of Historic Preservation, Department of Parks and Recreation, Sacramento, California.

La Peninsula. "Patron of the Coastside: Robert Mills, 1823–1897." May 1984.

Report on the Historical and Architectural Significance of the Robert P. Mills Dairy Barn. California Department of Parks and Recreation. June 1989.

Robert P. Mills' Spanishtown Ranch Cultural Landscape Report. California Department of Parks and Recreation. June 2004.

San Mateo (CA) Times. "Coast Barn on National Register List." 1989.

———. "Half Moon Bay Barn May Be Name Historic Place." 1989.

———. "Secluded Park Site." July 18, 1988.

3. Francis Beach

Azoran Brothers. "A Brief History of the Azores." Date unknown.

The Californians. "Azoreans to California." May/June 1987.

Coastside Comet (Montara, CA). "Death of Francis." October 22, 1920.

———. "Half Moon Bay Items." March 8, 1918.

———. "Joseph M. Francis Mourned by Many." October 22, 1920.

———. "Joseph M. Francis Succumbs to Long Illness." October 22, 1920.

Half Moon Bay Memories. "Fourth of July in HMB: The Way We Were." 1977.

Historical Resources Report. "Francis Building." May 10, 1981.

Peabody, Claire. *Singing Sails.* Caldwell, ID: Caxton Press, 1950.

———. "Then Three Times 'Round." *The Skipper*, March 1963.

"Portuguese in America." Thesis by Sandra Knight Wolforth, Florida Atlantic University, 1976.

San Francisco Chronicle. "Ill-Fated Ship *New York* a Total Loss." March 15, 1898.

———. "Rich Cargo of the Wrecked *New York*." March 15, 1898.

———. "Sinking in Her Bed of Soft Sand." March 16, 1898.

San Francisco Evening Bulletin. "Last of the Famous Ship *New York*." March 14, 1898.

San Mateo County and City Officials. Blue Book or State Roster. 1889–1928.

Wolforth, Sandra K. "The Portuguese in America." Master's thesis, Florida Atlantic University, December 1976.

4. Pomponio State Beach

Cutter, Charles. *Stories of Old Missions in California.* San Francisco, CA: Paul Elder & Company, 1917.

Goerke, Betty. *Chief Marin: Leader, Rebel and Legend.* Berkeley, CA: Heyday Books, 2007.

Marin (CA) Independent Journal. "Miwok Outlaw Known for Mayhem and Murder." February 7, 2012.

Masters, Ryan. "Finding Pomponio." September 30, 2019. https://ryanmasters831.com.

Milliken, Randall. *A Time of Little Choice.* San Francisco, CA: Balena Press, 1995.

La Peninsula. "Indians of San Mateo County." Winter 1973–74.

Sausalito Historical Society. "Drake Meets the Miwoks." October 2, 2019.

The Trail Companion. "Names on the Land." Fall 2000.
Warpaths to Peacepipes. "Miwok Tribe." January 16, 2018.

5. Pebble Beach

Alexander, Philip, and Charles Hamm. *History of San Mateo County.* Burlingame, CA: Burlingame Publishing Company, 1916.

Builders of a Great City: San Francisco's Representative Men. San Francisco, CA: San Francisco Journal of Commerce Publishing Company, 1891.

Ingersoll, Luther. *Memorial and Biographical History of the Central Coast of California.* Chicago: Lewis Publishing Company, 1893.

Kemble, John H. *The Panama Route.* Berkeley: University of California Press, 1943.

Lewis, Oscar. *Sea Routes to the Gold Fields.* New York: Alfred A Knopf, 1949.

Morrall, June. *The Coburn Mystery.* El Granada, CA, Moonbeam Press, 1992.

———. *Half Moon Bay Memories.* El Granada, CA: Moonbeam Press, 1878.

Postal Gazette (Melano, Switzerland). "Panama Route: 1848–1851." November 2006.

Santa Cruz (CA) Waves. "Collecting Ancient Rocks in Bloomers." February 11, 2015.

Tate, E. Mowbray. *Transpacific Steam.* New York: Associated University Presses, 1986.

6. Butano State Park

Alexander, Philip, and Charles Hamm. *History of San Mateo County.* Burlingame, CA: Burlingame Publishing Company, 1916.

Alley, B.F. *San Mateo County History and Biographies.* San Francisco, CA: B.F. Alley Publishing, 1883.

The Almanac (Pescadero, CA). "Logging in the Butano." October 29, 2003.

Cloud, Roy. *The Story of San Mateo County.* Chicago: S.J. Clarke Publishing, 1928.

Daily Journal (San Mateo, CA). "Purdy Pharis: Murder or Suicide." February 2, 2004.

Echo. "Purdy Pharis—Shingle King." April 1989.

Environmental Science Associates. "Pescadero-Butano Watershed Assessment." March 2004.

Gazette. "S.P. Pharis." March 17, 1773.

Half Moon Bay Review. "Sister Marie Elise McCormick." July 31, 2013.
————. "This Old House." October 9, 2002.
The Irish Story. "Great Irish Famine." October 18, 2016.
Los Angeles Times. "For Many, Irish Coffin Ships Lived Up to Their Name." September 3, 1995.
McCormick, Marty. *The Butano—1912.* Pescadero, CA: Self-published, 2012.
Times and Gazette (Redwood City, CA). "A Fatal Shot." March 8, 1884.

7. Pigeon Point Light Station State Historic Park

Alameda County Biographies. "Phineas F. Marston." December 10, 2001.
California State Parks. "Historic Structures Report: Pigeon Point Lighthouse." September 2012.
Carleton Historical Society. "Rise and Fall of Sheriff Winslow." April 28, 1995.
Daily (CA) Alta California. "Wreck of the Carrier Pigeon." June 8, 1853.
Houghton, Barbara. Interview with the author. February 23 and April 11, 2011.
Marston genealogy. Compiled by Nathan W. Marston. January 25, 1888.
National Park Service. "Historic American Buildings Survey." Fall 2002.
New York Daily Tribune. "Loss of the Carrier Pigeon." July 12, 1853.
San Francisco Call. "Phineas Marston's Will Invalid." November 8, 1896.
San Francisco Herald. "Loss of the Clipper Ship Carrier Pigeon." June 8, 1853.
San Mateo County (CA) Times-Gazette. "Naming of Pigeon Point." February 21, 1903.
Tuttle, Kathleen. *Sylvanus Marston, Pasadena's Quintessential Architect.* Santa Monica, CA: Hennessey & Ingalls, 2002.
U.S. Army and Navy Journal and Gazette. "The Army." February 22, 1868.
Weekly Mirror (Bath, ME). "Carrier Pigeon." January 1, 1853.
Williams, C. *History of Penobscot, Maine.* Cleveland, OH: Williams, Chase & Company, 1882.

8. Año Nuevo State Park

Angel, Myron. *History of San Luis Obispo County.* Oakland, CA: Thompson & West, 1883.
California Historical Society Quarterly. "The Steele Brothers, Pioneers in California's Great Dairy Industry." September 1941.
California State Parks. "Cultural History." 2015.

————. "San Mateo Coast Sector Volunteer Study Guide." January 2009.

Confederate Veteran. "Notable Events of the Civil War." January 1900.

Daily Alta (San Francisco) California. "Notes from Pescadero." May 30, 1867.

Guide to the Steele Family Collection. Santa Cruz Museum of Art and History, 2015.

Hearn, Chester. *The Last Great Battles of the Civil War.* Jefferson, NC: McFarland and Company, 1993.

Lighthouse Digest. "Memories of a Lighthouse Lookout Station." July 2008.

Point Reyes National Seashore Historic Resource Study. "Ranching on the Point Reyes Peninsula." N.d.

Postel, Mitchell. *San Mateo County: A Sesquicentennial History.* Belmont, CA: Star Publishing, 2007.

Sacramento (CA) Daily Union. "California State Dairymen's Association." June 3, 1876.

San Luis Obispo Country Magazine. "When Dairy Was Queen." Spring 2013.

San Mateo Genealogical Society. "Steele Brothers Dairies of Pescadero." February 2, 2015.

Smith, Arthur H. Interview with the author. Summer 2007.

"The Steeles of Año Nuevo." Compiled by Catherine B. Steele, 2000.

The Tribune (San Luis Obispo, CA). "Dairying Booms in SLO County after Great Drought of 1862–64." March 15, 2014.

World War II Magazine. "Japanese Subs Prowl the U.S. Pacific Coastline in 1941." July 1998.

9. Rancho del Oso State Park

The Almanac. "Sawmills Played a Key Role in Peninsula's Early Days." December 5, 2001.

Britannica. "Theodore Jesse Hoover—American Engineer, Naturalist and Educator." January 31, 2021.

California Historical Society Journal. "Mrs. Theodore J. Hoover (1872–1940)." September 1940.

Cox, Thomas. *Mills and Markets: A History of the Pacific Coast Lumber Industry.* Seattle: University of Washington Press, 1974.

Herbert Hoover National Historic Site. "Hulda Minthorn Hoover." October 25, 2018.

————. "Jesse Clark Hoover." October 25, 2018.

————. "Theodore Jesse Hoover." October 25, 2018.

National Park Service. "Historic American Landscapes Survey." July 29, 2013.

"Rancho del Oso—How it Was (1914–1945)." Manuscript by Hulda Hoover McLean, unknown source and date.

Santa Cruz Public Library. "A Walk Through Time: William Waddell." N.d.

Santa Cruz (CA) Sentinel. "Estate of Theodore Hoover Is Virtually a Paradise." October 20, 1928.

———. "Hulda McLean Writes Hoover History." August 27, 1967.

Semones, JoAnn. *Whalers, Wharves and Warfare*. El Cerrito, CA: Glencannon Press, 2017.

Stanger, Frank. *Sawmills in the Redwoods*. Redwood City, CA: San Mateo County Historical Association, 1967.

10. Wilder Ranch State Park

California State Parks. "Santa Cruz Program Manual." December 1999.

Coast View (Santa Cruz, CA). "Wilder Ranch." January 28, 2021.

Elliott, Wallace. *Santa Cruz County Illustrations*. San Francisco, CA: Wallace W. Elliott & Company, 1879.

Harrison, E.S. *History of Santa Cruz County, California*. San Francisco, CA: Pacific Press Publishing Company, 1891.

Livingston, Dewey. *A Good Life: Dairy Farming in the Olema Valley*. San Francisco, CA: Golden Gate National Recreation Area, May 1995.

National Park Service. "Historic American Building Survey." Fall 1989.

Office of Historic Preservation. California State Parks. "Villa de Branciforte." October 14, 2012.

Santa Cruz County History Journal. "Don Jose Antonio Bolcoff." 1997.

Santa Cruz (CA) Evening News. "Joaquin Castro Became Large Santa Cruz County Land Owner." October 17, 1936.

———. "Russian Was Last Alcade of Santa Cruz." October 15, 1957.

Santa Cruz History. "The Sailors." August 24, 2014.

Santa Cruz Life. "Turning Water into Milk." 2021.

Santa Cruz (CA) Patch. "Celebrate the 40th Anniversary of Wilder State Park." October 16, 2014.

Santa Cruz Sentinel. "Bolcoff, Moore, Doak Sawmill." September 3, 1950.

Santa Cruz (CA) Weekly Sentinel. "Deloss D. Wilder Is Dead." September 5, 1906.

11. Henry Cowell Redwoods State Park

Associated Press. "Henry Cowell Dead." August 4, 1903.

City of Santa Cruz Planning and Development Department Report. "Economic Development of the City of Santa Cruz: 1850–1950." October 20, 2000.

Cowell Historical Society. "Cowell Family." 2020.

Daily Alta California. "Lime Trade in Santa Cruz." June 18, 1855.

Friends of Cowell Lime Works (Santa Cruz, CA). "Who Was Henry Cowell." October 10, 2015.

Harrison, E.S. *History of Santa Cruz County.* San Francisco, CA: Pacific Press Publishing Company, 1802.

Maritime Heritage Project. "Timothy Herbert Dame." 2018.

Millard, Bailey. *San Francisco Bay Region.* San Francisco, CA: American Historical Society, 1924.

Mountain Parks Foundation (Felton, CA). "Henry Cowell Is a Wonderful Place." 2020.

Newsletter of the Friends of the Cowell Lime Works Historic District. "Lime Kiln Chronicles." Fall/Winter 2009–10.

Perry, Frank. *Lime Kiln Legacies: The History of the Lime Industry in Santa Cruz.* Santa Cruz, CA: Museum of Art and History, 2007.

San Francisco Call. "Jurors Acquit Leigh Ingalsbe." November 12, 1903.

Santa Cruz Magazine. "Henry Cowell: Enigmatic Figure of Santa Cruz History." 2010.

Santa Cruz Sentinel. "Cowell Lime Works to Be Added to National Register of Historic Places." May 19, 2007.

———. "They Made a Fortune in Limestone." January 5, 1986.

Santa Cruz Trains. "Curiosities: The Henry Cowell Lime & Cement Company." December 6, 2019.

S.H. Cowell Foundation (Santa Cruz, CA). "Henry Cowell and His Family (1819–1955)." 1989.

Warner, Samuel. *History of Wrentham, Massachusetts.* Boston: A.E. Foss & Co., 1890.

12. Seacliff State Beach

American Concrete Institute. "Summary of Proceedings of the 15th Annual Convention." June 27–28, 1919.

American Shipper. "San Francisco Shipbuilding Company." June 10, 2020.

American Society of Civil Engineers. "A Historical Landmark." May 2021.

American Society of Engineers. *Year Book of 1916.* New York: House of the Society, 1916.

Anchor Light (Alameda, CA). "Concrete Ships." September 2013.

Architect and Engineer. "Puffed Brick for Concrete." April 1916.

Daily News. "Noble Experiment in Cement Ships Sank." September 8, 2003.

Fougner, N.K. *Seagoing and Other Concrete Vessels.* London: Foowde, Hoddes and Staughton, 1922.

Heron, David. *Forever Facing South, the Story of the S.S.* Palo Alto. Santa Cruz, CA: Otter B. Books, 1991.

International Journal of Scientific and Engineering Research. "Low Cost Ferro-Cement." October 2015.

"Joseph Louis Lambot," Maison Lambot brochure. Summer 2020.

Nauticus. "Facts about Concrete Ships." November 30, 1918.

New York Times. "Big Concrete Ship Afloat in Pacific." March 15, 1918.

———. "Concrete Ship Has Trial." May 6, 1918.

San Jose (CA) Mercury News. "Oil Trail Leads to Cement Ship." September 6, 2006.

Santa Cruz County Plan for Seacliff Village. "How Did That Ship Get Here?" County of Santa Cruz. 2014.

Santa Cruz Sentinel. "Concrete Ship Remains a Central Coast Landmark." July 26, 2015.

Soundings (Boone, IA). "Cement That Floats." June 21, 2016.

U.S. Army Waterways Experimental Station Report. "Concrete Ships and Vessels: Past, Present and Future." October 1977.

ABOUT THE AUTHOR

Courtesy of Julie Barrow.

Author JoAnn Semones, PhD, is best known for her engaging series about shipwrecks at lighthouses along the Central California coast. The books were published by the Glencannon Press. They include: *Shipwrecks, Scalawags and Scavengers: The Storied Waters of Pigeon Point*; *Whalers, Wharves and Warfare: People and Events That Shaped Pigeon Point*; *Hard Luck Coast: The Perilous Reefs of Point Montara*; *Pirates, Pinnacles and Petticoats: The Shipwrecks of Point Pinos and Monterey Bay*; *Sea of Troubles: The Lost Ships of Point Sur*.

In her first book for The History Press, *True Tales of California Coastside State Parks*, JoAnn focuses on profiles of trailblazing pioneers connected to Coastside state parks. Each left a distinct imprint on specific properties and on the Coastside as a whole.

JoAnn's stories have appeared in a variety of history and maritime publications. She has made presentations before many history associations, educational organizations and civic and senior groups, and she has participated in special events at Coastside lighthouses, the historic Johnston House, Kohl Mansion and Villa Montalvo, and aboard the Liberty ship *Jeremiah O'Brien*.

JoAnn is featured in a video highlighting local maritime history that is part of a permanent exhibit, *Ships of the World*, at the San Mateo County History Museum. She is also a consultant for California State Parks and for the Coastside State Parks Association. For more information, visit her website at www.GullCottageBooks.com.

Visit us at
www.historypress.com